Anthology of Modern Chinese Poetry

Anthology

of Modern

Chinese

Poetry

Edited and

translated by

Michelle Yeh

Yale University Press

New Haven and London

Published with assistance from the Mary
Cady Tew Memorial Fund.

Designed by Sonia L. Scanlon
Set in Sabon type by Marathon Typography
Service, Inc., Durham, North Carolina.
Printed in the United States of America

Library of Congress
Cataloging-in-Publication Data
Anthology of modern Chinese poetry /
    edited and translated by Michelle Yeh.
        p. : ill. ; cm.
    "Published with assistance from the
Mary Cady Tew Memorial Fund"—
P. iv.
    Includes bibliographical references
and index.
    ISBN 0-300-05487-4 (cloth)
        0-300-05947-7 (pbk.)
    1. Chinese poetry—20th century—
Translations into English. I. Yeh,
Michelle Mi-Hsi.
PL2658.E3A57   1993
895.1'1508—dc20   92-16322
                    CIP

A catalogue record for this book is available
from the British Library.
The paper in this book meets the guidelines
for permanence and durability of the
Committee on Production Guidelines for
Book Longevity of the Council on Library
Resources.

10 9 8 7 6 5 4 3

Contents

Contents

Contents

Contents

Contents

Contents

Contents

Contents

Contents

Contents

Contents

Contents

Acknowledgments

The completion of this anthology would not have been possible without the generous support and assistance of many friends, colleagues, and institutions. John G. Ryden, director, and Ellen Graham, former senior editor, of Yale University Press first suggested an anthology to me. In selecting individual poets and poems, I consulted Yang Ze and found many of his ideas helpful. Kang-i Sun Chang read my proposal and gave me much-appreciated suggestions. William Moss and Zhang Lingxia helped me choose the poems of Shu Ting and Zhu Xiang, respectively. I thank them all.

Given the limited space of an anthology, I could not include all the poets or poems I would have liked. I am grateful to all the poets whose works grace the pages of this volume for their support and understanding. Some generously made their recent works available to me or suggested a few poems for inclusion; Ya Xian and Yang Ze helped me contact many others. Because of difficulties in obtaining permissions, I regretfully had to leave out two poets, Fang Si and Bei Dao.

The translations would not be what they are without the invaluable collaboration of Jeanne Tai on many of the Taiwan poets; I have learned a great deal about the art of translation from her. I am also indebted to Scott Ezell for his generous help with some of the younger poets. The contributions of Kari E. Lokke on Ya Xian, and Robin A. Stevens, Kirk Wulf, and Melinda Hansmire on a mixed group of poets are gratefully acknowledged.

If translation, by anyone's account, is an onerous and time-consuming task, working with someone else's translations requires even more patience and skill, which my editor, Mary Pasti, has in abundance. I have benefited enormously from her insightful comments, meticulous attention to detail, and unflagging enthusiasm. Any flaws that remain in the translations are solely my responsibility.

A substantial portion of the introduction was presented at the Humanities Institute, University of California, Davis, in spring 1991. I wish to thank the fellows of 1990–91, as well as Michael J. Hoffman and Kay Flavell, who contributed to the seminar discussion. I was fortunate to work with this group of fine scholars, whose comments encouraged me to pursue my ideas further and helped me refine them. I am grateful to the Council for Cultural Planning and Development and the Pacific Cultural Foundation, both in the Republic of China in Taiwan, for a translation grant and a writing grant, respectively, and to the University of California, Davis, for a number of research grants, which allowed me to take time off to complete this project.

My indebtedness to a large number of Chinese anthologies of modern poetry published in China, Taiwan, and Hong Kong is too immense to be adequately acknowledged here. One must be singled out, however, for its extraordinary scope and depth. The two-volume *Anthology of Modern Chinese Poetry* (*Xiandai Zhongguoshi xuan;* Taipei: Hongfan, 1990), edited by Yang Mu (C. H. Wang) and Zheng Shusen (William Tay), served me as a model of comprehensiveness.

Above all, I wish to thank C. H. Wang, whose support and encouragement has guided me through the various stages of the project. I hope this anthology is a worthy token of my esteem.

Introduction: From the Margin

A writer in the margins or completely outside his or her fragile community is all the more likely to express another possible community and to forge the means for another consciousness and another sensibility.
—Gilles Deleuze and Félix Guattari

To introduce an anthology of modern Chinese poetry with an explicit reference to its marginality may sound deprecatory. As I hope to demonstrate, however, marginality aptly characterizes the historical context in which modern Chinese poetry has developed over the past seven decades and defines the intellectual and artistic vantage point from which it is, and can be, most creative and powerful. I use marginality both heuristically and critically, to describe the sociocultural conditions in which the poetry is written and to provide a theoretical platform from which to study its dynamics. The concept evokes the departure of poetry from the central position it once occupied in Chinese society and implies, at the same time, its newly gained distance from the center, which has made possible a truly critical dialogue with that center.

Like the "pacesetters" described by some sociologists—people who, because they "become involved in any type of social mobility before it has become customary," are "on the borders between two . . . worlds without really belonging to either"—modern Chinese poetry is borderline.[1] It stands between traditional society, which is fast disappearing, and modern society, which is dominated by mass media and increasing consumerism.

Since the turn of the century, the social and political structure, educational system, and culture of China have been radically transformed. The republic founded in 1911 replaced millennia-old imperial rule; the abolition of the civil service examination in 1904—for which a command of the poetic art was desirable, if not required—closed the most important avenue of upward mobility; and extensive implementation of westernized education shifted the emphasis from the humanities to science and technology. Consequently, poetry lost its privileged position as the cornerstone of moral cultivation, a tool for political efficacy, and

1. Tamotsu Shibutani, *Social Processes: An Introduction to Sociology* (Berkeley: University of California Press, 1986), 314–15.

the most refined form of social liaison. It came to be viewed instead as a highly specialized, private, and socially peripheral pursuit. Although modern poetry was born in the New Literature Movement of 1917, whose primary impetus was "the larger social and cultural benefits literary innovation seemed to promise," rather than intrinsic aesthetic considerations, it was prose fiction that took on the grand mission of saving the nation and the short story writer and the novelist who spoke for society.[2] The traditional hierarchy, in which poetry is revered and prose fiction is deemed trivial, was reversed.

Although all contemporary cultural products have been commercialized as traditional society has disappeared, the rise of mass media (radio, films, television, videos) has widened the gap between elite culture—to which poetry has always belonged—and popular culture. Their audiences are vastly disproportionate in size. Short stories and novels, which to the Chinese are closer to popular culture, are less marginally situated than poetry. Contrary to the intention of its pioneers, modern poetry has not attracted a wide audience, despite the use of the vernacular as the new poetic medium—it is more easily understood and more popularist than convention-bound classical Chinese—and despite the wider accessibility of education. Ironically, modern poetry has been pushed to the margins of the world it helped create and usher in.

A New Orientation to Poetry

Déclassé in the old society and trivialized in the new, modern poets have been compelled to redefine their position and discover new roles. These concerns are consonant with, and were further reinforced by the emergence of, individualism in early modern China. It is no accident that many pioneers of modern poetry championed self-expression as the major, if not the only, goal of poetry. Hu Shi, in calling for "poetic empiricism" in the poem "Dreams and Poetry," insists on the uniqueness of individual experience. Romantic love, which was suppressed in Confucian ethics and was treated as a secondary topic in traditional poetry, has become a dominant theme, inviting an unprecedented range of expressions.

If self-expression is nothing new to traditional Chinese poetics, an

2. Marston Anderson, *The Limits of Realism: Chinese Fiction in the Revolutionary Period* (Berkeley: University of California Press, 1990), 25. See also Theodore Huters, "A New Way of Writing: The Possibilities of Literature in Late Qing China, 1895– 1908," *Modern China* 14.3 (July 1988): 243–76.

essential difference between classical and modern poetry lies in how the place of human beings in nature is perceived. One of the earliest modern poems at once echoes and negates the traditional view. Written in 1917, the year of the New Literature Movement, Shen Yinmo's (1883–1971) "Moonlit Night" reads:

> The frosty wind howls loudly,
>   The moon shines brightly.
> I am standing next to a tall tree,
>   But I am not leaning on it.[3]

The images—the moon, the tree, the wind, and the frost—are only too familiar to readers of traditional poetry. The presentation of nature as intimate (the closeness between the poet and tree), beautiful (the bright moon), and awesome (the cold wind) is reminiscent of much classical nature poetry. The last line, however, takes a radical turn. Shen's emphasis on difference rather than dissolution of difference, on distinction rather than blurring of distinctness, between human beings and nature, pronounces a new independence of the individual. If nature is still regarded as a companion, with appealing and not-so-appealing attributes, the poet suggests that although people are physically weaker than nature (intimated by the menacing wind and the tall tree), they are capable of achieving a nobility and grandeur of their own. The speaker's proud assertion of his independence testifies to the heroic potential of the individual.

The awakening to individuality has led to much intense self-analysis in modern Chinese poetry. Although sentimentalism derived from self-pity or self-affection occasionally makes itself felt, modern poetry is distinguished by its candid probings of the multiple psychological and existential dimensions of the self, its reflections, for instance, on the relations between love, beauty, truth, time, history, and oneself. The views of earlier and later poets have striking parallels. Yang Mu's "Lama Reincarnated" reaffirms a faith in compassion, wisdom, and peace despite rampant ignorance and violence. The persona of the six-year-old lama, embodiment of the childlike innocence and pristine clarity of which all humans are capable, resembles the little girl in Xu Zhimo's "On the Train," whose singing emancipates her fellow passengers from the consuming darkness of apathy and desolation. The brooding introspection

3. Sun Yushi, ed., *Readings of Modernist Poetry* (*Xiandai shi dao du*) (Beijing: Beijing daxue chubanshe, 1991), 24.

and the private images of Bei Dao's (b. 1949) "Days" bear an affinity
with those of He Qifang's "Sandstorm Days." Both Shang Qin's "Elec-
tric Lock" and Chen Feiwen's "Notes on Fleas on a Cat" reveal a far
more ambivalent attitude toward human nature. If Chen's bronze mirror
—to which the Buddhist nun's bald head is compared—reflects the per-
ishability and transience of human desires, Shang's image of all-embrac-
ing darkness suggests the human lack of self-reflexivity.

The last two poets' candid and detached probings into human exis-
tence were preceded in the work of Mu Dan. In "Self," Mu dissects
human existence with a surgeonlike precision, exposing its randomness
(the speaker happens to be born into a particular language and creed),
lack of autonomy (he uses conventional labels for things and emotions
that he has acquired unconsciously and uncritically), and self-deception
(his "glorious kingdom" is just a small shop). The concluding image of
a dream waiting for someone to dream it in another world does not
simply repeat the banal metaphor of life as a dream; it drives home the
point that our lives are run by linguistic and social conventions largely
beyond our awareness or control. Alerting us to the ever-present danger
of leading an unauthentic life, the poem is itself the product of intense
self-reflexivity and self-analysis.

The self in modern Chinese poetry is more often tragic than trium-
phant, possibly because of the marginal status of poetry and the poet.
Images of the odd person out, the aimless wanderer, the solitary traveler,
recur. It is significant that the traditional poet most often invoked by
modern poets is Qu Yuan (343?–278 B.C.), the prototype of the misun-
derstood writer and banished seer; and the star has come to symbolize the
modern poet, who is alienated from and at the same time transcends
the everyday world.[4] Frustration and disillusionment may also explain
the ubiquity of poems written in the elegiac mode, lamenting a person
(whether the poet or another person), an event, an age, or even a civili-
zation. Xu Zhimo's elegies on Katherine Mansfield and Thomas Hardy,
two writers whom he greatly admired, voice his bitter realization of the
irreconcilable conflict between reality and the ideal, between earthbound
mortality and transcendent immortality. Wen Yiduo's "Perhaps (A
Dirge)" suppresses only to reveal more clearly his painful sense of help-
lessness as a father. Presenting himself as omnipotent, he creates a
perfectly peaceful and harmonious shelter for his daughter, something

4. See chap. 2 of my *Modern Chinese Poetry: Theory and Practice since 1917* (New
Haven, Conn.: Yale University Press, 1991).

he could not do when she was alive. Equally moving is Dai Wangshu's quatrain on Xiao Hong the novelist. Conspicuous in the poem, which is entitled "By Xiao Hong's Tomb, an Impromptu," is the absence of any mention of death; it presents images associated with life instead: a bouquet of red camellias and Xiao's leisurely listening to the ocean tides. Yet the absolute separation between the worlds of the living and the dead is evident in the juxtaposition of the patiently waiting poet and the nonresponsive Xiao.

Going beyond the personal level, Wu Yingtao's "Ruins" mourns a war recently ended. Instead of rejoicing at the return of peace, the poet foresees the inevitable repetition of the same human mistake, symbolized by the new ruins and a new memorial statue. Gu Cheng's "End"—which stirred up a controversy in 1980–81 for comparing the Jialing River, a tributary of the Yangzi in Sichuan Province, to a soiled shroud— "records quietly" the tragedy in China's recent past. By depicting those who died in the Cultural Revolution as "giants" whose skulls are piled high on the riverbank, the "handsome green trees" as twisted in pain, and the moon as "hacked" and "buried" in thick fog, "The End" evokes the vast destruction wreaked on both humankind and nature.

The experience of deprivation or dispossession is not all negative. For modern Chinese poets, the loss of traditional status has brought a gain in freedom from poetic and critical conventions. Just as they champion the independence of the individual, they perceive poetry as self-sufficient, based on yet separate from, responsive to yet transcendent of, the external world. Early on we see this perception in an analogy of Xu Yunuo's: poetry is an embroidery of the "garden of the future." The handiwork symbolizes the imagination, capable of transforming drab surroundings. Xu also associates poetry with the realm of the creative and the sacred in "Poetry," with its forest of marvelous music where no humans tread, and in "A Word," with the discovery of a new, brighter world in love. Poetry is also the subject of contemplation in Feng Zhi's "Sonnet 27," which says poetry organizes and gives meaning to the raw material of life.

Later poets are markedly conscious of poetry as fictive discourse. Luo Zhicheng's "Love Poem" begins with "This is going to be a love poem— / A flower doesn't need to feel embarrassed / About its fragrance," and Xia Yu's "Can of Fish" concludes with a disclaimer of the title and a revision of the stated theme. Both are hyperbolically self-referential, making explicit the nature of the poem as a verbal composition, a fictive construction.

The freedom from literary and cultural conventions is also directly linked to experiments in poetic art. Among the early poets, Xu Zhimo and Wen Yiduo were most successful with their use of rhyme and regular form; Zhu Xiang and Sun Dayu (b. 1905) with the sonnet, both Petrarchan and Shakespearean; Zong Baihua (1897–1986) and Bing Xin with the miniature lyric, inspired by the short lyrics of Goethe and Tagore, Greek epigrams, and Japanese haiku; Lu Xun (1881–1936), Zhu Ziqing (1898–1948), and Xu Zhimo with the prose poem; Zhu Xiang, Sun Yutang (b. 1910), and Feng Zhi with the long narrative; Xu Zhimo, Wen Yiduo, and Dai Wangshu with the "circular form," which begins and ends with the same image or motif; and Ou Wai Ou (b. 1911) with typographical poetry.

Similar experiments are carried out today. Poets continue to favor the sonnet; Luo Fu and Xiang Yang have assayed ten-line versions, as in their respective poems *Death in the Stone Chamber* and "Autumn Verse." Most poets have written miniature lyrics at some point in their career; those of Fang Qi, Bei Dao, Xia Yu, and Gu Cheng are especially memorable. If Shang Qin writes prose poems that resemble those of earlier poets in their tendency toward introspection and self-confession, he imbues them with an absurdist atmosphere and a controlled, level tone. The poetic drama of Yang Mu, the pictorial and concrete poetry of Zhan Bing (b. 1921), Lin Hengtai, Bi Guo (b. 1931), and Bai Qiu, and the fugues of Ye Weilian are a few examples of recent attempts to develop new forms.

Marginality connotes a space in which to understand and reflect on traditions. Wen Yiduo's " Prayer" contains this refrain:

Please tell me who the Chinese are,
Tell me how to embrace memory.
Please tell me about the greatness of this people,
Tell me gently, do not speak loudly.[5]

The earnest and nostalgic tone with which the heroes and sages of the ancient civilization are evoked reveals a sense of loss and despair. Ya Xian's "On the Streets of China" expresses, under the casual, almost playful tone, an acute awareness of the contrasts between China's irrevocable past and its cosmopolitan, westernized present. If the recurrent image of the poet wearing corduroy hints at the superficiality of west-

5. *Collected Poems of Wen Yiduo (Wen Yiduo shi ji)*, ed. Zhou Liangpei (Chengdu: Sichuan renmin chubanshe, 1984), 209.

ernization, the conjunction between images of old China (the oracle bone script and the sacrificial tripod) and the West (the Muses) in the conclusion of the poem suggests, willy-nilly, a cultural blending.

In contrast to their traditional counterparts, modern Chinese poets are widely exposed to and, in many cases, seriously study foreign literature. Self-reflexivity is therefore not limited to their own literary tradition but extends to others. Yang Mu's "Three Etudes: The Snake" takes a fresh look at the biblical story of the Garden of Eden and offers a new reading of the relation of beauty to good and evil. Whether the snake is the archetypal evil and fallen angel of Western culture or the degenerate form of the dragon, the symbol of nobility and power in the Chinese tradition, the first-person speaker argues in its defense: "Beauty comes from time immemorial; / It is a mystical experience, fear-inspiring / With a touch of evil—but that is a misunderstanding." After thus freeing the creature from its conventional symbolism, the poet places it in the context of beauty. By using the third-person masculine pronoun in the first étude, the third-person feminine pronoun in the second, and the third-person reptilean pronoun (coined by the poet) in the last, the poem connotes that just as beauty is beyond gender, it is beyond the polarization of good and evil, beyond "tradition," "discipline," and "norms." Like the androgenous snake cum fallen angel, beauty embraces both good and evil and, in the final analysis, transcends them. "Heaven and earth were like a zebra"—the image of black and white stripes points to the coexistence and interdependence of apparent opposites. Unlike his biblical counterpart, the Adamic first-person speaker of the poem does not have to choose between good and evil, reason and emotion, obedience and knowledge, heaven and earth. Human civilization is the result of neither a fall from grace nor mechanistic evolution; it draws on the transformation of self-generating, self-transcending beauty, the principle of "continuous creation": "Heaven and earth were like a molt." The musical motif reinforces the theme of the poem, evoking as it does the characteristic absence of moral judgment in music and its resistance to being so judged—probably greater than for any other art form owing to its abstract nature.

Rebirth of the Individual: The People's Republic of China

Major forces, political and otherwise, have changed, or have sought to change, the milieu in which modern Chinese poetry is written. Although motivations have varied, attempts to demarginalize poetry have essentially been attempts to use extrinsic concerns to delimit and mold it.

From the early 1920s on, left-wing writers and critics actively promoted a literature purported to serve revolutionary needs, called "revolutionary literature," "proletarian literature," or, later, "socialist realism," and they repudiated individualism, "art for art's sake," and the "ivory tower" syndrome of bourgeois literature. Gan Ren and Han Shihang's defense of individualism in 1928 sought unsuccessfully to reconcile self-expression and realism. In 1932, Du Heng (under his pen name Su Wen) and Shi Zhecun (b. 1905), two editors of *Les contemporaines* (*Xiandai*), advanced the notion of "third-category literature"—written neither from the perspective of the gentry nor from that of the proletariat but instead from an objective critical perspective.[6] By arguing that literature could not effect social change and therefore did not have to be controlled, they tried to secure a marginal space where literature could be developed without political intervention.[7] Just as third-category literature was quickly dismissed by left-wing writers and critics in the 1930s, marginal literature has been suppressed in the People's Republic of China, where literature is required to serve the interests of workers, peasants, and soldiers. First formulated in Mao Zedong's "Talks at the Yan'an Forum on Literature and Art" in May 1942, the official literary policy leaves no room for ambiguity about priorities: of the two criteria for judging literary works, the political always overrides the artistic. Subsequent purges of writers—most extensively, the Anti-Rightist Campaign of 1957–58 and the Cultural Revolution of 1966–76—make the tragic case that political persecution virtually wipes out marginality. Ironically, because literature can influence minds and events, it is politically controlled and suppressed. Because it is made part of the dominant discourse in a totalitarian society, it is in effect silenced as a voice of the individual.

In this context, the publication of *Today* (*Jintian*), the first underground literary journal in the People's Republic of China, marks a watershed in modern Chinese poetry. *Today* was founded on December 23, 1978, its roots traceable to the late 1960s and early 1970s, when aspiring young writers and artists in Beijing—like Shi Zhi (b. 1948), Mang Ke, and Duo Duo—formed salons to discuss and experiment in

6. Anderson, *Limits of Realism*, 57.
7. On this point I am indebted to Wendy Larson's unpublished manuscript "Chinese Literary Modernism as a Discourse of Oppositionality."

literature and art.[8] Representing the generation of youth disillusioned by the senseless violence and wrenching hardship they witnessed and experienced during the Cultural Revolution, its editors consciously distanced themselves from the official ideology the better to reflect on and critique it. In the inaugural issue, they advocated the creative freedom of the artist and the autonomy of art.

The motif of silence is recurrent in many of the poems published in *Today*—by Shi Zhi, Bei Dao, Mang Ke, Shu Ting, Jiang He, and Tian Xiaoqing (b. 1953). China is a wasteland where stupefied silence reigns; the only sound is the unending dirge of rain (Duo Duo) or the monotonous sound of a key banging on a railing (Bei Dao). When Shu Ting said, "Alas, I can cry out at last," she spoke for all the poets of her generation who found that poetry was once again a vital way of reconstructing meaning in a world where meanings were uncertain and illusive, of creating private truths when public truths were tenuous and untenable.[9] The journal was closed down by the government at the end of 1980.

The songs of these poets were new and strange to the establishment, which called them Misty poetry (*Menglongshi*) in reference to their alleged obscurity and ambiguity. Menglongshi touched off a long series of heated debates in 1980–84 on the fundamental assumptions about the poet, the reader, and poetic art.[10]

The unfamiliarity of the Menglongshi style immediately raises the issue of readership. From the establishment point of view, if Menglongshi was hard even for the minuscule percentage of intellectuals to understand, how could it be understood by the masses? In other words, literary style is important not only as it relates to the content of a work but also in

8. For the historical development of *Today,* see Duo Duo, "The Buried Chinese Poets" ("Bei maizang de Zhongguo shiren"), *Pioneers* (*Kaituo*), 3 (1988): 166–68; Zhang Langlang, "The Sun Column" ("Taiyang zongdui"), *Today* (*Jintian*), n.s. 2 (1990): 63–67.

9. Shu Ting, "Dream of Returning Home" ("Guimeng"), in *Lyric Poems of Shu Ting and Gu Cheng* (*Shu Ting Gu Cheng shuqingshi xuan*) (Fuzhou: Fujian renmin chubanshe, 1982), 88.

10. For a comprehensive bibliography of articles and essays on Menglongshi, see *Documents on Literary Debates in the New Era* (*Xinshiqi wenyixue lunzheng ziliao*), 2 vols., ed. Yu Shiqian et al. (Shanghai: Fudan daxue chubanshe, 1988), 1: 138–45. For English sources, see William Tay, "'Obscure Poetry': A Controversy in Post-Mao China," in *After Mao: Chinese Literature and Society, 1978–1981*, ed. Jeffrey C. Kinkley (Cambridge, Mass.: Harvard University Press, 1985), 133–57, 301–4; Xiaomei Chen, "'Misunderstanding' Western Modernism: The *Menglong* Movement," *Representations* 35 (Summer 1991): 143–63.

that it reveals the attitude of the writer toward his or her readers. By indulging in obscurantism and thus failing to make their poems easily accessible, Menglong poets turned their backs on the people. Their poems blatantly deviated from the official ideology, which equates comprehensibility with artistic merit.

Inseparable from the issue of style was the issue of content. What the establishment probably found most unacceptable was the emphasis on individualism and self-expression and the implicit criticism of repression in Chinese society. Bei Dao's "Declaration—To Yu Luoke" proclaims the dignity of the individual: "In an age without heroes, / I only want to be a man." In a far more subtle way, his "Days" suggests the return of the individual by adopting an unmistakably personal perspective. The poem consists of a sequence of images describing the first-person speaker: jotting down notes on a favorite book, mailing a letter, looking at pedestrians, window-shopping, making a call in a public telephone booth, and so forth. By focusing on these prosaic yet personal, narrow yet subjective activities, the poem defines selfhood not in terms of social role and political ideology (which is customary, in fact mandatory in communist poetry) but rather in terms of the habits, likes and dislikes, and memories of the speaker. Self-perception and self-reflexivity surface in the two concluding images:

> I gaze at myself through the smoke
> In the dim mirror at the theater entrance.
> When curtains block off the noise of the sea of stars,
> I open the faded album and read the traces of words.[11]

From the murky fog and the darkness of the night emerges a self, solitary yet self-contained, with a rich world of memories and imagination.

From the establishment point of view, the individualistic content and form of Menglongshi was the direct result of the influence of Modernism. Modernism was also held responsible for the decadence, alienation, nihilism, escapism, pessimism, and retrogressive aestheticism that Menglongshi allegedly embodied. Shu Ting's "Assembly Line," for instance, laments the dissolution of individuality into numbing conformity from a factory worker's point of view. The establishment castigated it for giving an "unrealistic" portrayal of the socialist worker,

11. *Selected Poems of Bei Dao* (*Bei Dao shi xuan*) (Guangdong: Xinhua shudian, 1986), 20.

although Shu Ting argued that the poem was based on her own experience in a factory.[12]

In what way was the political establishment served by attributing these alleged characteristics of Menglongshi to undesirable Western influences? To admit that Menglongshi owed its rise to internal conditions more than to external forces was to admit the existence of spiritual crises —identity crises, the disintegration of values, alienation—comparable to those that gave rise to Modernism in the West during the second half of the nineteenth century. Although in the early years of the post-Mao era it was acceptable and even commendable for writers to portray negative aspects of social reality (hence "the literature of the scar" of 1977–80)—their portrayals being interpreted as the just denunciation of the extreme leftism of the Gang of Four—to continue to do so into the 1980s was not acceptable, for it implied the continued existence of problems that the government of the "new era" did not wish to admit. This refusal, indeed inability, to recognize historical reality made it virtually inevitable that an easy scapegoat would be found.

Experimental poetry groups and publications (most of which are published privately) have mushroomed since 1986; the poetry has been collectively labeled the poetry of the Newborn Generation.[13] Coming after the groundbreaking Menglong poets no doubt gives the younger poets a haunting sense of belatedness and a paralyzing anxiety of influence —hence their vehement reaction to and conscious departure from Menglongshi.[14] Instead of the intense lyricism and dense imagery (usually figurative) of Menglongshi, for example, they often employed the narrative mode, a low-key, matter-of-fact tone, and colloquial, nonfigurative language. The solitary hero or heroine in Menglongshi— Yu Luoke in Bei Dao's "Declaration," Zhang Zhixin in Jiang He's "Unfinished Poem," and the flying *apsara* in Yang Lian's "Dunhuang"—is superseded by the antihero, usually an urbanite trying to get by in an irra-

12. Shu Ting, "Life, Books, and Poetry—In Reply to Letters from My Readers" (Shenghuo, shuji yu shi—jian da duzhe laixin), in *Young Poets on Poetry* (*Qingnian shiren tan shi*), ed. Lao Mu (Beijing: Beijing daxue Wusi wenxue she, 1985), 11–12.
13. Other names used by critics to refer to the new wave of avant-garde poetry are "third generation," "fifth generation," and "avant-garde school." I am using Newborn Generation, for it seems to me the most commonly used and most straightforward designation.
14. The slogan widely circulated among younger poets is Pass Bei Dao (with *pass,* meaning "surpass," in English); it probably appeared around 1985. For a more detailed study of the Newborn Generation, see my "Nature's Child and the Frustrated Urbanite," *World Literature Today*, 65.3 (Summer 1991): 405–10.

tional, hostile universe. In Wang Xiaolong's "In Memoriam—Dedicated to My Father," the speaker realizes the frustration and anger his father must have experienced when he was alive ("you were smart / therefore you were incompetent"); he is able to identify with his father ("I am you") after having similar experiences. Knowledge and empathy do not resolve another kind of frustration, however: his realization comes too late to patch up his strained relationship with his father. The unbridgeable gap between the living and the dead is the ultimate frustration that he has no choice but to bear.

With its mundane setting—once, the speaker is anxiously waiting for a taxi to take him to his own wedding and, on another occasion, to take his wife to the hospital to give birth—Wang's "Taxis Always Come at Moments of Despair" deals with the same feelings of helplessness and futility as "In Memoriam." The comparisons of the bride and the groom to a pair of dolls and the groom's tie to a belt with which to hang himself reveal both an exasperating self-consciousness and a detached self-mockery that are rare in Menglongshi. In contrast to Menglong poets, who often project a vision of the ideal world or the desire to retrieve a perfect world (nature, childhood), the poets of the Newborn Generation tend to accept human limitations, even make fun of them, and to be resigned to an imperfect world.

In spite of some striking differences in language and style, poets of the Newborn Generation probably have more in common with their predecessors than they are aware of or care to acknowledge. For one thing, they share the same aesthetic consciousness about the autonomy of poetry and the same belief in creative freedom; for another, they use such similar themes as alienation, the quest for identity, and the intense exploration of the individual psyche. The line between Menglongshi and poetry of the Newborn Generation is not always easy to draw, and some of the Menglong poets—Yang Lian, Duo Duo, Wang Xiaoni—are closely associated with the younger poets. At a more fundamental level, both groups of poets consciously speak from the margin against a rigid, dogmatic society and, for their pains, have been harshly denounced by the establishment. In fact, many of the criticisms hurled at the Menglong poets are hurled at the Newborn Generation poets: they, too, are accused of nihilism, pessimism, individualism, and being influenced by Modernism. In addition, their poetry is repudiated as trivial and meaningless.

The marginal stance taken by the Menglong poets and the Newborn Generation is powerfully articulated in two poems: Bei Dao's "Life of an Artist" and Meng Lang's (b. 1961) "Survivor of This Century." The first poem depicts the first-person narrator in submission to authority figures, be they familial, legal, or medical. His mother tells him to buy some turnips, a traffic policeman yells at him on the street, and, after tripping on the street, possibly over the cane of a blind pedestrian, he is taken to a hospital:

So I become a model patient
Sneezing loud and clear
I figure out the mealtimes with eyes closed
Donate blood to bedbugs again and again
No time for sighs
Finally I, too, become a doctor
A large syringe in hand
I pace up and down the hallways
To while the night away[15]

The absurdist reversal of roles satirizes the system that subjects people to authority of various kinds and deprives them of freedom of choice—for example, by assigning jobs with no regard to ability or proclivity. Like the drunkard (earlier in the poem) who longs for the sea, a symbol of freedom and imagination, the artist is always at odds with society and is bound to be a marginal member of it. With an ironic twist of its title, the poem shows that the artist cannot have a purposive, fulfilled life in such a system.

Meng Lang's poem begins with these lines:

Learn to breathe untrue air
Before uttering
True words.

At moments like this I write poetry
And lie.
Those who live in the building
Are all my best friends.
It's a pity that I don't know any of them.

The poem ends with the speaker committing a symbolic suicide with a revolver:

I shall die truthfully
In the untrue air.[16]

15. *Selected Poems of Bei Dao*, 95–96.
16. Meng Lang, "A Survivor of This Century" ("Ben shiji de yige shengzhe"), in *A Survivor of This Century* (Guangxi: Lijiang chubanshe, 1988), 1–2.

The first two stanzas indicate a fundamental lack of trust and communication between people. The poet turns to poetry, where he can be true to himself, but he lies (or has to lie) when dealing with the world. The ambiguous juxtaposition of writing poetry and lying is a subtle subversion of the establishment's disapproval of the new poetry—from Menglongshi to the poetry of the Newborn Generation—as lies about the society when, in fact, the poetry is telling the truth. The choice for the poet, suggested by the ending of the poem, is between truth (of poetry) and death (of the poet's soul).

For the poets of the Newborn Generation, as for the Menglong poets, poetry is both a symbolic and a real means of territorializing the marginal space that provides poets with a critical distance from the dominant discourse of the political-cultural establishment. A fine distinction between the two groups lies in degree: the younger poets probably feel an added sense of marginality in the increasingly commercialized society of post-Mao China. Popular love poetry, published by official presses, appeals to a large audience and makes a considerable profit, but most of the Newborn Generation poetry is published in mimeographs by individual poets (or groups of poets) and is of extremely limited circulation.[17] Caught between political dogmas and the commercialization of poetry, Meng Lang, in "Winter," implies the poet's rejection of both:

> Poetry points to poetry itself.
> I throw a jacket on,
> Go through the empty lot,
> And disappear from this city. A bronze statue—
> I cannot put my foot in it.
> Poetry points to the heart.
> The four walls are white as snow;

17. A few examples of commercial success are the cassette of *Selected Lyrics of Zhang Jianhua* (thirty thousand copies in the first edition), which was released in spring 1990, and the cassette of Xi Murong's poetry, whose sales set records for poetry in Taiwan in the early 1980s. Another mainland poet, Liang Xiecheng (b. 1938), is well known for his first book of love poems, entitled *The Swaying Tree of Lovesickness* (*Yaoxie de xiangsi shu*); published in 1987, it has sold more than twelve thousand copies. His second volume, entitled *The Flavorful Fruit of Love* (*Duo wei de aiqing guo*), was recently advertised in the poetry journal *Greenwind* (*Lufeng*, January 1991) as written specifically for "young boys and girls who enter the world of love for the first time." The latest success is the pat, sentimental poetry of Wang Guozhen, who has published two volumes since 1990.

The vacant room is habitable—
Quite the contrary. Let us walk through
This empty lot, through this city,
Through poetry itself.

Then we will settle down,
Make a fire, take off our jackets
And our underwear,
And expose our bodies. We will face poetry
Or turn against it.[18]

Even though the poet walks away from the bronze statue, an image evocative of the official ideology, the vacant room and the empty lot, suggesting the emptiness of contemporary culture, are also unsuitable for living. The search for a space outside the city (with its statues, vacant rooms, and empty lots)—within the individual psyche or in the mythological past of China, to name two tendencies among the poets of the Newborn Generation—represents the poet's staunch defense of poetry.

Social Conscience: Taiwan

In postwar Taiwan the situation is immediately more complex and more subtle than in the People's Republic of China owing to significant differences in their political and cultural makeup. The Nationalist government first articulated its literary policy during the Chongqing period in September 1942. Its spokesman was Zhang Daofan (1896–1968), director of the Propaganda Bureau, who listed six don'ts and five dos in his "Literary Policy That We Need." The six don'ts are (1) do not focus on the dark side of society; (2) do not instigate class hatred; (3) do not reflect pessimism; (4) do not express romantic sentiments; (5) do not write meaningless works; and (6) do not express incorrect consciousness. The dos are (1) create our national literature and art; (2) write for the common people who suffer the most; (3) write from the standpoint of the nation; (4) produce works from reason; and (5) use realistic forms.[19] As Christopher Lupke points out, Zhang's article was pub-

18. Meng Lang, "Winter" ("Dongtian"), in *Seventy-Five Contemporary Chinese Poems* (*Dangdai Zhongguo shi qishiwu shou,* mimeograph), ed. Bei Ling and Meng Lang (Beijing: N.p., 1985), 37–38.
19. The article originally appeared in the first issue of *Cultural Vanguard* (*Wenhua xianfeng,* Chongqing) in September 1942. It is reprinted in *Essays on Native Literature* (*Xiangtu wenxue taolun ji*), ed. Yu Tiancong (Taipei: Yuanliu, 1978), 815–45.

lished four months after Mao Zedong's "Yan'an Talks," and the two concur significantly in content.[20]

After the move to Taiwan in 1949, the Nationalist government controlled literature to a high degree by sponsoring literary activities and censoring the mass media. In April 1950 the Chinese Literature and Art Awards Committee was set up; the next month the Chinese Literature and Art Association was formed; and they were soon followed by the Young Writers' Association and the Women Writers' Association. In addition, the few newspapers in the early postwar period were mostly owned and run by the government, and books by many Chinese writers who stayed on the mainland and by some foreign writers were labeled subversive and banned. Through these and other means, the Nationalist government created a dominant discourse geared to the restoration of the Chinese mainland to Nationalist rule and the legitimation of the Nationalists as the true heirs to Chinese culture, not the Communist usurpers.

Many poets in postwar Taiwan sought to create an alternative discourse. Granted, their poetry displayed a wide array of styles and themes. When collectively viewed, however, their works contrast sharply with the mainstream discourse promoted by the Nationalist government, particularly from the 1950s through the early 1970s, in challenging the anticommunist ethos of the time and in engaging in the avant-garde. The poetry can be described as Modernist to the extent that, like its Western counterpart, it stresses formal unity, employs complex metaphors and symbols, values such effects as irony, ambiguity, understatement, and paradox, and articulates a generally critical view of modern society and culture. The profound sense of alienation and dispossession that characterizes Modernist literature in the Western tradition is also found in modern Chinese poetry of the period.

Ji Xian, one of the pioneers of avant-garde poetry on Taiwan, has compared himself to a deserted island, a solitary wolf howling in a barren wilderness, a tree that bears no fruit, a youth whom the world jeers at for trying to pluck the stars from the sky, and a spectator who refuses to participate. He bemoans and at the same time celebrates the marginal position he occupies; he criticizes modern culture, which dehumanizes and commercializes art, and revels in seemingly trivial things. Probably

20. I am indebted to Christopher Lupke's unpublished paper "Nationalist Literary Policy, Cold War Ideology, and the Development of the Culture Industry in Post-War Taiwan," presented at the Conference on Politics and Ideology in Modern Chinese Literature held at Duke University, Durham, N.C., in October 1990.

for the first time in modern Chinese poetry a poet finds sheer delight in describing the translucent, peach-colored body of a bee in the sunlight; the "peacefulness, dignity, and beauty" of a dead fly; a princesslike mosquito on a worn paint brush; a dignified gecko; and the fantasized metamorphoses of clouds in the sky and smoke from a pipe.[21] In identifying with insects and smoke—of peripheral interest and nonutilitarian significance—Ji Xian implicitly questions conventional values and perspectives.

Ya Xian's work resounds with an equally critical note. The prefatory poem to his collection harks back to Gérard de Nerval's "Christ to the Olive Trees" ("Le Christ aux oliviers"), which portrays modern man as "pushed over the brink by his quest for intellectual and metaphysical knowledge" in a society so dominated by greed and materialism that "the sense of the sacred" is destroyed.[22] Identifying the poet with Christ, Ya Xian laments the total loss of interest in spirituality in modern society, even in a negative form. For the poet even crucifixion is impossible:

But the price of poplar is going up!
Steel nails are drilled into skyscrapers,
And people have totally lost any interest
In being pharisees
Or Saint-Simonians
To spit curses at his not-so-high nose.[23]

Christ, who represents the hope of redemption, also appears in Ya Xian's "Abyss," where he is rejected by modern people, who suffer from moral cowardice, emotional anemia, and vulgar hedonism. "Salt," set during the transition from imperial to republican China in the early twentieth century, makes a poignant comment on social injustice. By juxtaposing the poor peasant woman both with Dostoevsky and with the indifferent angels, the poem expresses the pathos of human suffering and at the same time suggests its ultimate futility and raises doubts about the hope of redemption.

Also written in the late 1950s, Luo Fu's poem sequence, *Death in the Stone Chamber,* criticizes the stifling of spiritual and imaginative life by the hypocrisy and emptiness of conventional religion and by the

21. Ji Xian, *Self-Selected Poems of Ji Xian (Ji Xian zixuan ji)* (Taipei: Liming wenhua, 1978), 15, 32, 179, 326.
22. Kari E. Lokke, *Gérard de Nerval: The Poet as Social Visionary* (Lexington, Ky.: French Forum, 1987), 126.
23. *Collected Poems of Ya Xian (Ya Xian shi ji)* (Taipei: Hongfan shudian, 1981), 2.

shadow of imminent death (the poem was written while he was stationed on Jinmen, the target of heavy bombings by the Communists at the time). The first-person narrator of the poem repeatedly describes himself as an injured tree. He is also the cross that bears Christ, which religious people spit on. Ironically, positive images of life give way only to death: a grain of wheat is murdered by the "storage house of abundance" (sequence 6); the kernel of a fruit "dies in forgiveness" (15); and a newborn baby "smiles at the grave" (36).[24] By the same token, his "Song of Everlasting Regret" rewrites the classic poem of tragic romance by portraying the Chinese emperor as hedonistic, selfish, and cowardly.

When we consider the military service of poets like Luo Fu and Ya Xian, who were at one time officers under the Nationalist government, the critical thrust of their works takes on a keener edge of irony. Their use of religious allusions and imagery, often of foreign origin, in voicing their social criticisms can be interpreted as a veiled satire against the Nationalist government, which promotes its anticommunist discourse with a religious fervor; yet anticommunism, the poets suggest, is a debased religion, devoid of spiritual depth or promise of salvation.

Alienation is found not just in those poets who emigrated to Taiwan from the mainland in 1949. Bai Qiu, for instance, is a native Taiwanese whose work in the 1960s and 1970s conveyed that same theme with images of a restless moth killed by a candle flame, a drifting leaf, a bird separated from its flock, a solitary wanderer, a man echoing only himself, a grain of sand, a speck of dust, and a silent gecko—all profoundly peripheral. Poetry is a cocoon that shelters the poet from a "stubborn," indifferent world, and poems are leaves on trees, although no one appreciates them or even knows of their existence. The only glimpse of hope takes the shape of a "virgin land on the sea":

We are the blueprints for the kingdom of poetry and music;
We are the pioneers in the virgin land on the sea.[25]

24. See *Luo Fu's Death in the Stone Chamber and Critical Essays* (*Luo Fu shishi zhi siwang ji xiang guan zhongyao pinglun*), ed. Hou Jiliang (Taipei: Han'guang wenhua shiye, 1988).
25. Bai Qiu, "Compass" ("Luopan"), in *Only When the Wind Blows Does One Feel the Tree's Existence* (*Feng chui cai gan dao shu de cunzai*) (Taipei: Chunhui congshu, 1989), 42.

Bai Qiu envisions an ideal world beyond conventional space and time. This type of projection is common in the works of many poets in postwar Taiwan.

If many poets in Taiwan, as on the mainland, were dismayed by their peripheral status, they were simultaneously exalted by the infinite possibilities of artistic expression. While writers on the mainland were suppressed, poets in Taiwan in the three decades after 1949, in contrast, did much to refine the vernacular into a versatile and effective poetic medium. If 1957 marked the inauguration of *Poetry Monthly,* the clarion of official ideology on the mainland, 1953–54 saw the founding of the Modernist school, the Blue Star Poetry Club, and the Epoch Poetry Club in Taiwan, which produced some of the best modern Chinese poets.

In the 1970s a different response to the marginalization of poetry arose in Taiwan, represented by the controversy over modern poetry in 1970–74 and the full-fledged Native Literature Movement of 1977–79. The movement centered on a configuration of issues concerning the nature and function of literature, including the question of Chinese (and Taiwanese) identity versus foreign (predominantly Western) influence and the precedence of Realism over Modernism. Although the Nativists objected to Modernism for its obscure style and negative tone and subject matter, at a deeper level they were reacting to the marginal status of literature, poetry in particular, in the twentieth century. Their accusations of aestheticism and escapism boil down to the perception that, in the hands of Modernist poets, poetry is as much marginalized as it is marginalizing; it is alienated and alienating from society at large. The Nativists held the Modernists largely responsible for creating their own undesirable situation.

In essence, the Native Literature Movement bespoke an effort to change the peripheral status of poetry by making it socially relevant and engaged; the ultimate goal was to demarginalize poetry and reintegrate it into the mainstream of social discourse by adopting a realist (and supposedly more accessible) approach and dealing with topics of contemporary social and political import. Poets, in other words, would assume the central role of social critics (or, at the very least, concerned citizens). This hidden agenda led the Nativists to valorize dichotomies like native versus foreign, Chinese versus Western, literature as a catalyst of social enlightenment (if not social progress) versus literature as self-expression, and Realism versus Modernism. The rigidity of their categories is apparent in their prescriptive tone and in the analogies they employed repeatedly in condemning the Modernists: sickness versus health, impotency versus virility, decay and death versus growth and vitality.[26]

The paradox of the controversy remains: to the extent that the Nativists tried to create an alternative discourse to resist the dominant discourse manipulated by the Nationalist government, they were actually in agreement with the Modernists. However, by insisting on a causal connection between the economic infrastructure and the cultural superstructure of society, the Nativists repudiated the Modernists as accomplices to the government in allowing Taiwan to become an economic and cultural colony of the United States and Japan. They consequently blunted the critical edge of Modernist poetry, either knowingly or unknowingly. The satire underlying the juxtaposition of warfare and love making in Yu Guangzhong's "If a War Is Raging Afar" and "Double Bed," for instance, was disregarded, and the poems were disparaged as decadent, selfish, and even pornographic. The use of Modernist techniques was categorically correlated to slavish imitation and treacherous complicity with the colonizer (the United States). Modernism was all too quickly dismissed as an element of the moral malaise of Western society, rather than its diagnostician.

The real difference between the Nativists and the Modernists, it seems to me, lies in their response to the marginalization of poetry. If the Modernists used their marginal status to sustain artistic freedom and social criticism, the Nativists sought to change the marginal status of poetry once and for all. Defining the value of poetry in terms of social conscience, the Nativists believed that poetry would be demarginalized once it proved itself to be an aid to the improvement of social conditions. Ironically, in their overzealous attempt to justify the narrowly defined social role of poetry, they referred to Zhang Daofan's "Literary Policy That We Need," hence taking the side of the Nationalist government, which they were opposed to otherwise.

Besides the crucial failure of the movement to make fundamental changes in the cultural and historical conditions under which modern poetry is written, we must consider whether the socially engaged poetry advocated by the Nativists fulfilled its function of social criticism any better than Modernist poetry did. Whereas the Modernists perceived themselves as marginal, the Nativists took on the self-assigned task of

26. See, for instance, the essays by Yu Tiancong, Chen Yingzhen, and Tang Wenbiao in A Critical Survey of Modern Literature (Xiandai wenxue de kaocha), ed. Zhao Zhiti (Taipei: Yuanjing chubanshe, 1976), and in Essays on Native Literature, ed. Yu Tiancong.

speaking for the disenfranchised members of society. Victims of the system appear frequently in their poetry: young girls sold into prostitution; underage workers in underground factories; latch-key children; aborigines, who suffer from economic and social disadvantages; young men from the country who are led astray in the city and end up in prison; adolescents under pressure to pass the high school entrance examination, and so on. If the speaker in the Modernist poem identifies with the victim, his or her counterpart in Nativist poetry poses as the reporter or spokesperson for the victim. The danger in speaking for the disadvantaged is that representation often turns out to be underrepresentation or even misrepresentation; speaking for others is often a way to suppress their right to speak for themselves. By implicitly standing apart to observe and sympathize, Nativist poets impose their own perspective on the victims and unwittingly reiterate or even reinforce stereotypical images.

For instance, the trite contrast between the pure, innocent country and the corrupt, materialistic city is made ad nauseam; the aborigines are without exception portrayed as "primitive" and close to wild nature, and the women are usually self-sacrificing wives and mothers. Although one editor praises the depictions of the "traditional virtues of Chinese women," this kind of remark ignores the implicit exclusion of a more representative sampling of modern women and the subtle perpetuation of conventional gender roles.[27] Similarly, poems about prostitutes ultimately do a disservice to the people whom the Nativists intended to save. If they exhibit sincere sympathy for the women and genuine anger at the injustice done to them, all too often these emotions are diffused by clichés and sentimentality—say, by identifying the women with Mother Nature.

If the highly condensed language of Modernist poetry disrupted and subverted the dominant discourse, the figures of speech in Nativist poetry tended to subvert its purported function as social conscience. Nativist poetry fell short of its goal not because it was realist but because it was not realist enough. Instead of presenting reality in its fullness, no matter how unspeakable, the Nativists often resorted to shallow romanticism and a figurative language that hid and distorted reality.

Since the late 1970s, particularly from the 1980s on, others have

27. Wu Sheng's comment on Duo Si's "Doing Laundry" ("Xiyi"), in *Selected Poems of Taiwan, 1983 (1983 Taiwan shi xuan)* (Taipei: Qianwei chubanshe, 1984), 23. The speaker in the poem is a wife-mother who willingly gave up her career to better take care of her husband and children.

undertaken to demarginalize poetry, too, though their efforts have been far less concerted and controversial than the push by the Native Literature Movement. If the Nativists sought to change the marginal status of poetry in ideological terms, the recent demarginalizers have tried to bring poetry into popular culture through commercial and other means. In the hope of narrowing the gap between elite culture and popular culture, poetry has been presented in new forms in the mass media to make it more accessible. In the mid-1970s composers had already begun to set modern poems to popular tunes; folksingers, mostly with a college background, sang them, and poets gave public recitations. In the past six or seven years, the innovations have become more diversified. Poems are performed with sound effects, slides and films, pantomime, comic dialogue, and dance. Poets have written lines for advertisements of commercial products, and poems have decorated a variety of items, from the more traditional bookmarks and stationery to T-shirts and pillows.

The reasons for the increasing commercialization of poetry in contemporary Taiwan are complex. One is that a growing number of poets have become editors of the literary supplements of major newspapers, where they are in an advantageous position to bring poetry to a wide readership.[28] To some extent, the attempts to popularize poetry can also be related to the escalating interest in Postmodernism among Taiwan's intellectuals since the 1980s. The Postmodernist dismantling of literary conventions, the intentional blurring of the distinction between high and popular cultures and the demarcations between disciplines, appeals to some poets because it seems to offer a way out of the backwater to which poetry has been relegated since the early twentieth century.

The most significant reason for integrating poetry into the consumer market is, arguably, the Native Literature Movement of the 1970s. As some of its most vocal and influential spokespersons concede in retrospect, the movement did not succeed in bringing literature in general and poetry in particular into the mainstream discourse; endowing poetry with an explicitly didactic intent did not attract more readers. If anything, it accelerated the trivialization and commercialization of literature in the 1980s.[29] If poetry is seen and heard in more forms and

28. To name a few, Ya Xian is an editor of *United Daily News* (*Lianhe bao*), Yang Ze of *China Times* (*Zhongguo shibao*), Luo Zhicheng of *China Times Evening Post* (*Zhong shi wanbao*), Mei Xin (b. 1935) of *Central Daily* (*Zhongyang ribao*), Xiang Yang of *Independence Evening Post* (*Zili wanbao*), and Liu Kexiang of *China Times*.
29. See Cai Yuanhuang, "A Retrospect on the Native Literature Controversy" (Pingyi xiangtu wenxue lunzhen"), *China Times* (*Zhongguo shibao*, Taipei), literary supple-

perhaps more often than ever before, the tendency toward fragmenta-
tion and decontextualization—as when a poem is partially quoted on a
bookmark or printed on a T-shirt or when it appears as a space filler in
the hotchpotch of a literary supplement—brings it into closer com-
plicity with the consumer market. Although exaggerated for the purpose
of parody, what Xi Xi (b. 1938), the noted short story writer and poet,
says about Hong Kong newspapers applies equally well to Taiwan:
"Never mind those prose pieces; even when it comes to poetry, it works
the same way. If the square [of a newspaper column] needs seventeen-
and-a-half lines of poetry each day, the poets are sure to submit a poem
of seventeen-and-a-half lines each day—not a line too long or a line too
short."[30] In direct proportion to the expansion of the market, the site
of poetry as an alternative discourse and critical space seems to be
shrinking. Xia Yu's and others' refusal to let commercial publishing
houses handle their poetry volumes, instead designing and publishing
their own, can thus be seen as an oblique comment on, and an act of
resistance against, the commercialization of poetry.

Women's Poetry

Just as women have been traditionally marginalized in Chinese society,
barred from participating in the sociocultural sphere on equal terms
with men and deprived of physical, intellectual, and social autonomy,
so, too, have women poets occupied a peripheral place in the literary
canon, the range of their poetry bound by literary conventions and
moral constraints narrower and more rigid than those for men. It is
from this peripheral position, then, that modern women must speak
out.

Among the early modern poets, a number of women, most notably
Bing Xin, Lin Huiyin, and Chen Hengzhe (1893–1976), broke new
ground. They freed themselves from the *wanyue*, or "feminine," tradi-
tion in Chinese poetry, in which typically a woman sits alone in her
boudoir, perhaps leaning on the windowsill overlooking a beautiful yet
confining garden, and pines for her absent lover or husband or wallows
in melancholy over lost love. Bing Xin widened the vista, introducing

---

ment, Jan. 4, 1991; and Chen Yingzhen, "The Necessity of New Readings and
Discourses" ("Xin yuedu han lunshu zhi biyao"), *China Times*, literary supplement,
Jan. 6, 1991.
30. Xi Xi, "Glass Slippers" ("Boli xie"), in her collection of short stories *A Girl Like
Me* (*Xiang wo zheyang de yige nuzi*) (Taipei: Hongfan shudian, 1984), 58.

such magnificent images as the roaring sea and the vast starry sky, which are virtually unknown to traditional women's poetry. She also addressed a broader range of topics, including the relations between mothers and daughters, human beings and nature, ideals and reality, and poets and the world.

In the poetry Lin Huiyin wrote in the 1930s, we also see the woman as at once freer, more complex, and in more control of her physical and emotional life than before. One of her last poems, entitled "Life," written in 1947, begins:

> Life,
> You are a tune;
> I am the singer,

and goes on to compare the narrator to a traveler and life to "fields, forests, and mountain peaks."[31] The implication that she decides where she goes in life and takes responsibility for her self-fulfillment generally reflects the burgeoning individualism of the 1920s, the May Fourth era, and specifically relates to the new definition of womanhood in the whole modern period.

Compared with the May Fourth era, in the last three decades the number of women poets and their output have increased considerably, making an outstanding contribution to the corpus of modern Chinese poetry. Although the spring scene in Rong Zi's "I Walk through the Season" is a familiar one, no sentimentality is associated with the passage of spring, which is the standard metaphor for youthful beauty and romantic love in traditional poetry. The speaker's determination to walk through life resolutely endows her with a strength and confidence unseen in the past.

Rong Zi's "My Dresser Mirror Is an Arch-Backed Cat" repudiates the stereotypical identification of a woman with a mirror and its underlying implications of the simultaneous subservience (to give men pleasure) and vanity (to win male attention and affection) in women's exclusive focus on physical attractiveness. Whereas traditional poetry by both sexes often portrays a woman literally from the angle of the dresser mirror, the speaker in Rong Zi's poem rejects her mirror as confining and as incapable of reflecting her true self, which is more beautiful, more gentle, and more complicated than her image. The shift in the role

31. Lin Huiyin, "Life" ("Rensheng"), in *Collected Poems of Lin Huiyin* (*Lin Huiyin shi ji*) (Beijing: Renmin wenxue chubanshe, 1985), 65, 66.

of the mirror, from active (a cat's ever-changing pupils) and manipulative (fate locks her up) in the first three stanzas to passive (a stranded cat that has lost its rhythmic gait) and illusive (a dream) in the last stanza, reverses the relation of the speaker to the mirror: she is now freed from its dominance.

The self-representation of women in modern Chinese poetry can be further illustrated by a brief look at how they deal with romantic love. Although their poems are by no means limited to this subject, it is a revealing index. They write about a wide range of experiences. Both the joy and pain of love find moving expression in Xiong Hong's work. The courage to endure pain in a relationship is depicted in "Envoi," and the courage to cross the boundary between life and death is treated in "Death." If "Envoi" is universal, showing the supreme power of love, "Death" is distinguishable from traditional poetry, where perseverance in love is more often justified on moral grounds than based on self-knowledge. Xiong Hong's "Bound" describes yet another type of courage, one that enables the speaker to walk out of a nonreciprocal relationship, although her alternative, total isolation from the world, may not be a viable solution, either.

In "To the Oak Tree," Shu Ting compares the man to an oak and herself to a ceiba tree (the source of kapok). If one symbol is common in traditional poetry, the other certainly is not. The usual image of a woman as a vine clinging to a stout tree—where the tree is clearly the center, the vine the margin—or to a steadfast rock can be traced to the *Book of Songs* (*Shijing*), of the eleventh to sixth centuries B.C.

In contrast, Shu Ting depicts the woman as a tree that is both the same as and different from the oak tree—as strong, but differently shaped and colored. The role for women that she presents is equal and complementary to men's instead of dependent and submissive:

I would have to be a ceiba tree by your side,
Standing with you—both of us shaped like trees.
Our roots hold hands underground,
Our leaves touch in the clouds.
When a gust of wind passes by
We salute each other
And not a soul
Understands our language

. . .

We share cold waves, storms and thunderbolts;
Together we savor fog, haze and rainbows.
We seem to always live apart,
But actually depend upon each other forever.[32]

In the same way, the female speaker in Shu Ting's "Goddess Peak" chooses to have "a good cry on the lover's shoulder" rather than be immortalized in a stone statue of unrequited love; articulation is contrasted with silence, freedom of expression (and movement) with immobility.

Wang Xiaoni is another young poet in China who creates new images of women. Her "Holiday, Lakeside, Reverie" also gives an interesting twist to the traditional rendition of women. The woman's skirt flapping up in the wind is reminiscent of "boudoir poetry," where it is usually the spring wind that exposes the female body, thus suggesting the woman's suppressed sexual desire. Wang's poem also addresses suppression, but of a broader nature—we see the triumph of individual liberty, symbolized by the woman's hair flying in the wind, over public opinion, which is represented by the watchful eyes around her.

With the advent of Menglongshi, a large number of women poets, including Zhai Yongming, Lu Yimin (b. 1962), Tang Yaping (b. 1964), and Zhang Zhen (b. 1951), concerned themselves with intense introspection and the search for self-identity. The image of night appears frequently in their poetry; away from the prying eye of the sun, they have a symbolic open space where they are temporarily released from all inhibitions and can express themselves freely. The female speaker in Zhai's "Let Me Tell You" satirizes the still-prevalent expectation that a woman be a "little lover," who knows "how to smile / Bravely and calmly" and for whom "shallowness is paradise." The frustration and anger aroused by such stereotypes of women is vented more explicitly in her "Mother," where the speaker watches herself being ground to pieces in the mill of time. The ambivalence she feels toward her mother comes from the pain, loneliness, and "misfortune" shared by all women:

Nobody knows how I love you. The secret
Comes from part of you. Like two wounds, my eyes stare at you.

The deeply tormented female voice is not at all like the tender, affectionate one in Bing Xin's "Paper Boat—Sent to Mother," written six decades ago.

32. Shu Ting, "To the Oak Tree" ("Zhi xiangshu"), trans. Edward Morin et al., in *The Red Azalea: Chinese Poetry since the Cultural Revolution* (Honolulu: University of Hawaii Press, 1990), 102.

Probably the boldest and most ingenious subversion of gender stereotypes is seen in Xia Yu's work. Many of her poems poke fun at the role traditionally assigned to women. In "Jiang Yuan," for instance, she rewrites the ancient legend of the mother of Hou Ji, the ancestor of the Zhou people, by shifting the focus to the woman. In the original poem in the *Book of Songs,* Jiang Yuan recedes into the background once she gives birth to the hero. By attributing such cultural and social systems as language, clan, and kingdom to the natural outgrowth of a woman's sexual desire and her equally instinctive drive for self-perpetuation, rather than to male intelligence and conquest, the poet demythologizes the notion that life and creativity derive from a male divine source.

"Common Knowledge" is another of her poems that satirizes male-oriented stereotypes of women. The flowing syntax—it contains one complete sentence consisting of four verbal and adjectival phrases—and the unitary structure, that is, the absence of stanzaic division, contrasts sharply with the hidden dichotomies at the semantic and perceptual levels. The regularity of a woman's body, described in the first three lines, is diametrically opposed to the irregularity of her mental and emotional state, in the last three. Biologically stable and predictable, a woman is not stable and predictable otherwise. Like a snake, she launches sudden attacks. The affinity is reinforced by her knowledge of the language of the snake. Because snakes are mute and have no capacity for verbal expression, "the snake's language" thus suggests something outside human, specifically male, understanding. It intimates women's mysterious and—through its evocation of the Garden of Eden—treacherous nature.

The irony underlying the title of the poem is central to the theme: it is "common knowledge" that women are unfathomable, potentially dangerous, and unreliable. Who is the knowledge common to? To men. The title exposes the totalizing nature of a patriarchal concept, which treats a prejudice as if it were objective and universal. The contradictory assumptions—that a woman is biologically predictable and mentally and emotionally unpredictable—reveal misogyny inherent in the male perception of the opposite sex.

Whether women's criticisms of patriarchy appear in love lyrics, confessional poems, satires, or parodies, they indicate an attempt to broaden the scope of poetry and introduce new ways of reading and writing it. Women's poetry is inseparable from other modern Chinese poetry as a marginal discourse.

For the poet, marginalization results in a profound sense of loss and alienation—loss of traditional status and alienation from the dominant social discourse. In Taiwan and China, where society is increasingly commercialized and consumer-oriented, the continued marginalization of poetry is probably inevitable and irreversible. Although the advance in democratization in recent years has given poets in Taiwan an unprecedented freedom of expression, the pressure of commercialization has also gained strength. The danger of sacrificing the integrity of art for marketability already exists, probably more in prose fiction than in poetry. In China, a society still in the initial stage of developing a consumer society, repressive policies are a constant force against literary creation. The revival of *Today* in Norway in 1990 and the founding of the poetry quarterly *First Line* (*Yihang*) in New York in 1987, bespeak an effort on the part of Chinese writers in exile to carve out a marginal space in which to interact with writers in their homeland as well as other Chinese communities in the world.

Marginality, as we have also seen, is not without its rhetorical, as well as ideological, advantages. The autonomy that comes with marginality leaves poets alone to search for their own rules, thus not only making experimentation possible but also ensuring the intellectual and artistic distance necessary for engaging in a truly critical dialogue with the dominant society. The poems included in this volume speak amply for the artistry and intellectual acumen that represent modern Chinese poetry at its best.

Note on the Translation

For various historical reasons, English readers more often associate Chinese poetry with the classical period than with the modern period. Classical poetry, which has dominated English translations of Chinese literature, dates from at least the eleventh century B.C.; modern poetry did not emerge until the first decade of the twentieth century. The Imagist movement launched by Amy Lowell and Ezra Pound in the early 1910s popularized classical Chinese poetry in the English-speaking world. Not only did Pound and Lowell translate it rather freely, but Pound's Modernist poetics, which has exerted considerable influence on later American poets, partly drew on his "discovery" of classical Chinese poetry. Although modern Chinese poetry was translated at least as early as the 1930s, it remains a relatively new subject to Western readers, and relatively few works have been translated. Therefore, it may be useful to comment on some of its linguistic and poetic characteristics.

Unlike its classical counterpart, modern Chinese poetry does not conform to a regular pattern that dictates the number of lines in a poem and the number of characters in a line. Most modern poems are written in an irregular form, although the quatrain and, less frequently, the terset and the couplet are common stanzaic divisions, as demonstrated by the poems in this volume. The leading Crescent poets—Xu Zhimo, Wen Yiduo, and Zhu Xiang—are particularly well known for their use of regular forms imported from the European tradition, like the sonnet and blank verse, as well as such exotic forms as the rondeau. My translations abide by the original forms of the poems, the only change being the arrangement of the lines on the page. Whereas Chinese poems published in China before 1949 and in Taiwan even now run vertically, as in the classical period—written top to bottom, right to left—they have to run horizontally in English. For samples of Chinese poems in their original form, see the appendix to my *Modern Chinese Poetry: Theory and Practice since 1917* (New Haven: Yale University Press, 1991).

Another distinguishing feature of modern Chinese poetry is that it does not follow traditional prosody. The musical effect is created by the sounds of the words, the arrangement of the lines, and the flow of sentences. Exceptions occur when poets adopt a regular form with a prescribed rhyme scheme, as Feng Zhi does with sonnets, or when they choose rhymes to achieve a songlike effect, as Yu Guangzhong does in

"Four Stanzas on Homesickness." In translating these poems, I have not reproduced the rhymes because they would sound stilted and forced.

Modern Chinese poetry employs the current vernacular, not formal, classical vocabulary and syntax. Like classical Chinese, modern Chinese is an uninflected language, often unspecific in tense, number, and subject of a sentence. Compared with its classical counterpart, however, modern Chinese has far more polysyllabic words, and its syntax resembles English.

To give an example, the last stanza of Hu Shi's "Dreams and Poetry" reads:

zui guo cai zhi jiu neng
ai guo cai zhi qing zhong
ni buneng zuo wode shi
zheng ru wo buneng zuo nide meng

Here is a literal translation:

getting only then know wine strong drunk
love only then know love heavy
you cannot make my poem
just as I cannot make your dream

And here is my translation:

Only one who has been drunk knows the strength of wine;
Only one who has loved knows the power of love.
You cannot write my poems
Just as I cannot dream your dreams.

Although the first two lines have no explicit subject, English syntax requires one. Given the generalizing nature of the statement, the universal "one" seems apt. For the same reason, I have adopted the present tense throughout the poem, except in the first two lines of this stanza, where the complement *guo*, indicating a completed act, lends itself to the present perfect tense. Other choices concerned the emphatic adverb *cai* (only), the adjectives "strong" for wine and "heavy" for love, and the verb "make" for poems and dreams. The final rendition takes English syntax, idiom, and economy of expression into consideration.

Modern Chinese poetry exhibits a wider range of syntactical versatility than classical poetry, being unrestricted by formal requirements. Whereas a line in a classical poem tends to be a complete unit of thought, enjambment is far more pervasive in modern poetry and is sometimes pushed to the extreme. A case in point is Yang Mu's "Let the Wind Recite," where the first fifty lines are, strictly speaking, one subjunctive clause beginning with "If," the first word of the poem; the main clause does not appear until line fifty-one, and then it runs on for thirteen lines. The highly convoluted syntax connotes the tortuous path of a romance and the faithful perseverance of the speaker; the long-delayed completion of the sentence mirrors the unfolding and cyclical pattern of the seasons, for the poem begins and ends with spring.

Shang Qin's "Faraway Lullaby" begins with an adverb, "languidly," the remaining fifty-six lines being but one long sentence, suggestive of a meandering lullaby. In contrast, Xia Yu's "Hibernation" is an incomplete sentence; its two stanzas present two prepositional phrases, both beginning with "In order to." The exact syntactical parallelism between the stanzas and the suspension of the rest of the sentence intimate the paranoia of the speaker, who is so busy preparing herself for love, for the anticipated coming and leaving of a lover, that she is never *in* love. I have kept the original syntax with a few necessary modifications.

The diction of modern Chinese poetry ranges from the archaic to the literary, the dialectal, and the colloquial. Nor is it uncommon to find a mixture of classical and colloquial diction or to come across a direct quotation from a classical poem. In a few cases, the intentionally jarring juxtaposition of archaic and colloquial words conveys irony or humor. Li Jinfa's "Thou Mayest Come Naked," for instance, uses the Chinese equivalent of "thou" instead of "you." Fang Qi's "Winter Curfew" begins each line with "Dost thou know." After much deliberation, I decided to keep some archaisms in the hope of preserving a sense of the original style.

Modern Chinese poetry may also include names, words, and even lines in foreign languages, including English (see, for example, poems by Xin Di, Qin Zihao, Ji Xian), French (Li Jinfa), Latin (Yang Ze), and Japanese (Yang Mu and Zhang Cuo). Poets in Taiwan and China have recently used scientific symbols and computer codes and have even invented esoteric signs.

Choices about diction go beyond individual words in Guan Guan's "Lotus Flowers," which represents a creative use of measure words. Chinese has not only the equivalents of "piece" (as in "a piece of paper") and "mug" (as in "a mug of soup") but many other measure words as well, such as *ge* for person and *duo* for flower. In Guan's poem, measure words customarily used for a body of water (as in "a lake of water" and "a pond of water") are used for "mud" and "buildings": "lakes of

mud" and "ponds of buildings." The unconventional and understand-
ably confusing concatenation suggests a Daoist-Buddhist view of contin-
uous or cyclical transformation (lakes—mud—plots—flowers—swamps—
ponds—buildings—houses—flowers) on the one hand and implies on the
other hand a critique of the dominance and even destruction of the nat-
ural world by artificial constructs. I have tried to preserve the originality
of the diction as much as possible.

Punctuation, a Western import, is used with less precision than in
English. Chinese poets often use commas, for example, where English
writers would use semicolons or periods. I have changed the punctua-
tion rather freely to conform to standard English usage. Chinese poets,
especially the earlier ones, are also prone to use exclamation marks,
along with such exclamatory words as *ah* and *oh*. For the most part, I
have changed the exclamation marks to periods and deleted the *ah*s and
*oh*s, which in English would sound ostentatious and sentimental. Some
of the Chinese poems are not punctuated. With a few exceptions, I have
added punctuation marks to aid readability. In Fang Qi's "Composition,"
Shang Qin's "Fugitive Sky," and several of Luo Fu's and Xia Yu's poems,
among others, I have left out the punctuation to convey the experi-
mental or idiosyncratic quality of the original. For similar reasons, I
have capitalized the first word of each line of most poems, although
there are no equivalents for capital and lowercase letters in Chinese.

Modern Chinese poetry is an exploration and development of formal,
musical, syntactic, and semantic originality. My objective in rendering
the poems into modern-day American English is to give readers a sense
of their original form, rhythm, diction, and ever-elusive style without
sacrificing readability.

The selection of poems was based on artistic merit and contribution
(or potential contribution) to the poetic medium. Poetry is an art, a
unique form of self-expression, and a powerful indicator of the quality
and texture of a culture. The poems translated here represent the achieve-
ments and innovations of modern Chinese poets. Because popularity can
be machinated by political, commercial, or other means—we have seen
those forces at work in the history of modern Chinese poetry—it is not
a valid or sufficient criterion for literary value. I have not hesitated to
include poets who may not be popular or even well known and to
exclude officially sanctioned poets despite their contemporary fame. My
hope is to give a general picture of the development of modern Chinese
poetry and to foster an appreciation of the fine, imaginative work that
has been done.

All of the translations are based on the Chinese originals as they appear in individual poetry collections and, occasionally, general poetry anthologies and poetry periodicals. I have indicated the date of composition or initial publication of each poem when possible. Where neither piece of information was available, the poems are arranged to the best of my knowledge in the order they first appeared.

The pinyin romanization system is used throughout. For poets who wrote in China before 1949 and who write in Taiwan, the Wade-Giles romanization of their names is added in view of their previous or preferred usage in English.

Anthology of Modern Chinese Poetry

Hu Shi

(Hu Shih, 1891–1963)

Hu was born in Anhui and received his Ph.D. in philosophy from Columbia University. He held such prominent positions as president of Beijing (Peking) University and ambassador from the Republic of China to the United States. The "father of modern Chinese poetry," he first advocated vernacular poetry in his "Eight Don'ts" in 1917 and published the first volume of modern Chinese poetry, *Experiments,* in 1920.

The afterword to "Dreams and Poetry," first published in *New Youth* in 1921, states: "This is my 'poetic empiricism.' To put it simply, even dreams must be based on experience, let alone poetry. The biggest problem with some poets these days is that they like to write poems that have no basis in experience." The poem "Flowers in a Vase" was written for Lu Xiaoman, the second wife of Xu Zhimo. The Lion in the poem by that name was Xu Zhimo's favorite cat, which Xu gave to Hu as a gift.

DREAMS AND POETRY

All are ordinary experiences,
All are ordinary images;
By chance they surge into a dream,
Turning out many an original pattern.

All are ordinary feelings,
All are ordinary words;
By chance they encounter a poet,
Turning out many an original verse.

Only one who has been drunk knows the strength of wine;
Only one who has loved knows the power of love.
You cannot write my poems
Just as I cannot dream your dreams.

October 10, 1920

FLOWERS IN A VASE

I fill a vase with flowers and cancel an outing—
I do not intend to grieve for plucked flowers.
I wonder if candlelight and incense
Are like the beating wind and battering rain.
—Fan Chengda [1126–93], "Flowers in a Vase"

Neither afraid of wind and rain
Nor envious of candles and incense,
I care only for the flower picker
And take delight in being near her.

Petals fall one by one.
Please ask her to save them
And send them to the one in her heart
As a wordless letter.

June 6, 1925

LION—REMEMBERING ZHIMO

Lion lies behind me—
A bundle of softness refusing to budge.
I am about to push him away
When I remember my deceased friend.

As I pat the snoring cat,
Two tears wet my sleeve:
"Lion, sleep tight—
You, too, have lost a good friend."

December 4, 1931

Xu Yunuo

(Hsü Yü-no, 1893–1958)

A native of Henan, Xu was a member of the Literary Research Society
and held various editorial and teaching positions, including stints as the
editor of the literary supplement of *Xiamen Daily* and as the principal
of the Lushan high school. Under the Communist regime, he was a rep-
resentative to the People's Congress and a member of the Chinese
Writers' League. The following poems are all selected from his 1923
volume, *Garden of the Future*.

LONGING

Sobbing must be the sound of longing; why do I hear sobbing when I
  miss you?
The taste of longing must be sour; why does my heart sour when I miss
  you?
The path of longing must be dark; why do I feel drowsy when I miss
  you?
On the dim, old path of memory I am traveling aimlessly.

April 7, 1922

SOUND OF THE NIGHT

In the dark, lonely night
Nothing is visible,
Only a rustling—the sound of time eating life.

April 14, 1922

GARDEN OF THE FUTURE

Sitting on a soft prairie, I unfold my dream like an old rag:
This is my work! Carefully I embroider patterns more beautiful, fresher,
  and more becoming to prepare for the future.
This is the garden of children.

May 3, 1922

LITTLE POEMS

1

What is a dream? What is reality?
Just a demarcation in human memory.
When you are here, you must leave there.

2

What is life? What is death?
Just a limitation in human perception.
When you are here, you cannot know there.

3

What we know and imagine is just a dream.
Reality is what we cannot imagine and know.

May 6, 1922

POETRY

Carrying these strange little poems,
I enter the forest slowly.
Silent birds nod to me,
Tiny bugs glance at me.
I enter the dimmer and deeper woods
And lay the strange things on wet grass.

Behold! In the forest
Insects stretch out their heads in turn;
Young leaves open their eyes one after another.
Music is wondrous and confusing,
Here, there, everywhere, in the forest,
Weaving with the mysterious yarns of poetry.

May 8, 1922

A   WORD

Cupid gave me a word—
Dumb, hard, and thorny.
I turned it around and examined it
But could not find its use.
So I put it on a bench by a sunny window.

During the quiet night,
When only nightingales cried,
A shaft of white light radiated from the bench—
I found a new world there
In this dark, lonely tangle.

May 10, 1922

Xu Zhimo

(Hsü Chih-mo, 1897–1931)

Born into a wealthy family in Zhejiang, Xu attended Hujiang University in Shanghai, Beiyang University in Tianjin, and Beijing University in 1915–18. He received a B.A. in history from Clark University (Massachusetts) in 1919 and an M.A. in economics from Columbia University in 1920. In 1921–22 he studied at King's College, Cambridge, where he started writing poetry. Xu founded the Crescent Society in 1923, which included such prominent writers as Hu Shi, Liang Shiqiu, Wen Yiduo, Lin Huiyin, and Sun Dayu. He published the literary supplement of the *Beijing Morning Post,* called *Poetic Engravings,* with Wen Yiduo and was editor in chief of the literary journal *Crescent Monthly.* In 1931, Xu died in an airplane crash in Ji'nan, Shandong, when he was en route from Shanghai to Beijing University, where he held a teaching position.

In one elegy translated below, Xu addresses Katherine Mansfield (1888–1923), the English short-story writer, whom he met in London in July 1922. Because of her failing health, the meeting lasted only twenty minutes. She died six months later in Fontainebleau. Xu visited her grave there in April 1925. The "poet who died on a voyage" is Percy Bysshe Shelley (1792–1822), who drowned near the Bay of Lerici, in Italy. Xu wrote another elegy to Thomas Hardy (1840–1928), the English poet and novelist.

Sayonara, a group of eighteen poems, is titled in the Japanese for "good-bye." The poems were written in May 1924, when Xu accompanied Rabindranath Tagore (1861–1941) on a trip to Japan following his visit in China. The Fusang Sea mentioned in the first poem is the Japan Sea. According to Chinese mythology, Fusang is a sacred tree from which the sun rises each morning. In early Chinese historiography, Fusang refers to an island to the east of China, later identified with Japan.

ELEGY FOR MANSFIELD

Last night in my dream I entered a dark vale
And heard cuckoos crying tears of blood amid lilies.
Last night I dreamed I ascended a mountain peak
And saw a gleaming tear falling from the sky.

In the suburbs of ancient Rome, there is a grave;
In it lies a poet who died on a voyage.

A century later, the wheels of Hades' chariot
Rumbled in the grove at Fontainebleau.

If the universe is a machine,
Why do ideals shine before our eyes like lamps?
If all things manifest truth, goodness, and beauty,
Why doesn't the rainbow stay in the sky?

Although you and I met only once,
Those twenty minutes are immortal.
Who could believe your heavenly presence
Is forever gone from this dewy world?

No! Life is but a dream of substance;
The fair soul is forever in the Lord's keeping.
A thirty-year sojourn is like a night-blooming cereus;
Through tears I see you return to the Celestial Palace.

Do you remember our London pledge, Mansfield,
That this summer we'd meet by Lake Geneva?
The lake always holds the reflection of snow-capped Mont Blanc—
When I look at the clouds, my tears fall.

That year, when I first came to understand the message of life,
I was struck, as if in a dream, by the solemnity of love.
Enlightenment about life lies in mature love;
Now, faced with death, I see the bounds of life and love.

Compassion is an unbreakable crystal;
Love the only path to realizing life.
Death is a grand, mysterious crucible
That forges the spirits of us all.

How can my condolences fly like electric sparks
To touch your soul in the distant sky?
I send you my tears with the wind—
When can I shatter the gate between life and death?

March 11, 1923

SAYONARA

1

I remember the sunrise over the Fusang Sea,
    Spreading like gold over the water.
I remember the islands in the Fusang Sea,

Floating like emeralds on the water—
      Sayonara!

2

Sailing on gentle waves,
  I spot old-style fishing boats here and there,
Like a flock of carefree seabirds
  Perching on the glittering waves at sunset—
      Sayonara!

18

It is above all the gentleness in lowering her head,
  Like a waterlily too frail to withstand the cool breeze.
Bidding farewell, bidding farewell,
  There is sweet sorrow in her "Farewell"—
      Sayonara!

May 1924

BUILD A WALL

You and I must never desecrate that word.
Let us not forget our vow before God.
I want your most tender love
To wrap around my heart like plantain peel
And your love as strong as pure steel
To build a wall in the flux of life.
Let the autumn wind cover the garden with sere leaves,
Let termites eat away carved pillars a thousand years old.
Even if a lightning bolt shattered the universe one day,
It could not shatter our freedom behind the wall of love.

August 1925

CORAL

No need to expect me to speak,
  My heart's sunk to the bottom of the sea;
No use beckoning to me again,
  For I can reply no more

Unless, unless you, too, would come
  To this world surrounded by coral reefs;
In the quiet moment when the sea wind subsides,
  You and I would exchange our sighs.

1926

A CHANCE ENCOUNTER

I am a cloud in the sky,
By chance casting a shadow on the ripples of your heart.
  No need to be surprised,
  Even less to rejoice—
The shadow vanishes in a wink.

You and I met on the sea at night;
You had your direction, I had mine.
  You may remember,
  Better yet forget—
The light emitted at the moment of encounter.

May 1926

BROKEN

1
Sitting on a deep, deep night,
A dim glow at the window,
  Dust balls rolling
    Down the alley:
I want to compose a broken, broken tune
With the dull tip of my pen
To express my broken thoughts.

2
Sitting on a deep, deep night,
The night chill at the window chinks,
  Jealous of the warmth fading from the room,
    Does not forgive my limbs:
I'll use my drying ink to sketch
Some broken, broken patterns,
For broken are my thoughts.

3

Sitting on a deep, deep night,
With grotesque shadows around me:
   Withered trees
    Screech on the bank of an icy river
     And gesture in wild despair,
Like me in my broken, broken consciousness
Trying to rebuild a broken world.

4

Sitting on a deep, deep night,
I reminisce with my eyes closed:
Ah, when she was still a cool white lotus
   In the morning breeze, delicate beyond compare.
But I am neither sunshine nor dew;
All I have is my broken breath
   Like the mice locked up in the wall,
Scuffling about, chasing after darkness and the void!

1927

THOMAS HARDY

Hardy, world-weary, life-weary,
   This time has no need to complain.
Has a black shadow covered his eyes?
   Gone, he will show his face no more.

Eighty years are not easy to live.
   That old man, he had a hard time.
With heavy thoughts burdening him,
   He could not let go morning or night.

Why did he leave sweets untasted
   And comfortable couches unused?
Why did he have to choose a gloomy tune to sing
   And spices that burned his tongue?

He was born a stiff old man
   Who loved to glare at folks.
Whoever he looked at got bad luck—
   No use begging mercy from him.

He loved to take the world apart;
  Even a rose would be ruined.
He did not have the gentle touch of a canary,
  Only the queerness of a night owl.

Strange, all he fought for was
  A little freedom of the soul.
He didn't mean to quarrel with anyone;
  To see truth was to see it clearly.

But he was not without love —
  He loved sincerity and compassion.
They say life is a dream;
  Still, it shouldn't be without comfort.

These days you blame him for his regret,
  Blame him for his thorny words.
He said optimism was the face of a corpse
  Made up with powder and rouge.

This is not to give up hope;
  The universe will go on.
But if there is hope for the future,
  Thoughts cannot be taken lightly.

To uphold the dignity of thought,
  The poet dared not relax.
He lifted ideals high, his eyes wide open,
  As he picked at life's mistakes.

Now he's gone, he can no longer speak.
  (Listen to the quietness in the wild.)
Forget him if you will.
  (Heaven mourns the demise of a sage.)

February 1928

SECOND FAREWELL TO CAMBRIDGE

Softly I am leaving,
  As I softly came;
I wave my hand in gentle farewell
  To the clouds in the western sky.

The golden willow on the riverbank
   Is a bride in the sunset;
Her luminous reflection in the ripples
   Is swaying in my heart.

Plants in the soft mud
   Wave in the current;
I'd rather be a water reed
   In the gentle river of Cam.

The pool in the elm shade
   Is not clear but iridescent;
Wrinkled by the swaying algae,
   It settles into a rainbowlike dream.

In search of a dream? With a long pole,
   Sail toward where the grass grows greener;
In a skiff loaded with starlight,
   Sing among the shining stars.

But I cannot sing tonight;
   Silence is the tune of farewell.
Summer insects are quiet for me, too;
   Silent is Cambridge tonight.

Quietly I am leaving,
   As I quietly came;
I raise my sleeve and wave,
   Without taking away a whiff of cloud.

November 6, 1928

ON THE MOUNTAIN

All's quiet in the courtyard,
   Except for a lingering urban ditty;
Pine shadows have woven a rug—
   Look, the moon is bright.

What is it like, I wonder,
   On the mountain tonight:
There must be the moon and pines, too,
   And quietness, only deeper.

Xu Zhimo

I wish I could climb on a moonbeam
  And turn into a puff of wind
To awake the pines from their spring hangover
  And let them sway gently on the mountain.

I'd blow off a fresh green needle
  And let it fall by your window;
Soft as a sigh—
  It wouldn't startle you in your sleep.

April 1, 1931

ON THE TRAIN

There are all ages and all trades on this train:
Bearded men, unweaned babies, teenage boys, merchants, and soldiers.
There are all the poses, too: leaning, lying down,
Eyes open or closed, or staring out the window at darkness.

The wheels grind out refrains on the steel tracks;
No stars in the sky, not a lamp along the road,
Only the dim lights on the bus reveal the passengers—
Faces young and old, all fatigued.

Suddenly, from the darkest corner comes
A singing, sweet and clear, like a mountain spring, a bird at dawn,
Or the sky lighting up over a vast desert,
Golden rays spreading to distant ravines.

She is a little child, her voice released in joy.
On this shadowed journey, at this dim hour,
Like a swollen mountain spring or a morning bird in ecstasy,
She sings until the bus is filled with wondrous melody.

One by one the passengers fall under its spell;
By and by their faces glow with delight.
Merchants, officers, the old and the young alike—
Even the sucking baby opens its eyes.

She sings and sings until the journey is brightened,
Until the fair moon and the stars come out from behind the clouds,
Until flowers on branches, like colored lanterns, vie in beauty,
And the slender grass rocks light-footed fireflies.

April 1931

Wen Yiduo

(Wen I-to, 1899–1946)

Wen Yiduo is the pen name of Wen Jiahua. A native of Hubei, Wen participated in the May Fourth Movement while he was a student at Qinghua University. In 1922–25 he studied English literature at Colorado College in Colorado Springs and Western painting at the Art Institute of Chicago before he moved to New York, where he published his first volume of poetry, *Red Candle*, in 1923. From the time he returned to China in mid-1925 to his death, he held a number of university positions, including the chair of the Chinese departments at Qinghua and Southwest United universities. The year 1928 marked not only the publication of his second, influential volume of poetry, *Dead Water*, but also his complete shift of literary interest to Chinese classics. On July 15, 1946, he was assassinated for his outspoken criticism of the Nationalist government and expressed sympathy for the Chinese Communist Party.

Wen was the leading theoretician of the Crescent school. His emphasis on the visual, musical, and architectural beauty of poetry led to many experiments with poetic form. The poet wrote "Perhaps" for his young daughter, Liying, who died of illness in 1926. He arrived home too late to be with her at the end. "Paper gold," gold nuggets of paper—sometimes along with paper money, paper furniture, paper houses, and paper clothes—is burned in sacrifice for the dead in hopes that they can use the supplies. The red beans of the eponymous sequence of forty-two poems are traditionally called the beans of lovesickness. The poems were written for Xiaozhen, Wen's wife, during his stay in the United States.

REMORSE

A romantic life
Is *love* written on the water;
It vanishes even as it is being written,
Stirring up undercurrents of pain.

COLORS

Life was a worthless sheet of white paper.
Green has since given me growth,
Red has given me love,
Yellow has taught me loyalty,
Blue has taught me nobility,
Pink has brought me hope,
Gray has brought me sadness.
To complete the picture,
Black will add death.

I have grown fond of my life
Because I love its colors.

RED BEANS

7

My heart was an empty city without guards.
One midnight it was ambushed by lovesickness.
My heart
Could do nothing except surrender;
I hoped
He would retreat once he'd done pillaging.
Who could have known that he would occupy it permanently
And build palaces and walls?

10

We have become one!
Our union
Is at least as perfect as the earth.
But you are the Eastern Hemisphere
And I am the Western Hemisphere;
With garnered tears
We have created the Pacific Ocean,
Which now keeps us apart.

13

After all, I am a man.
When we are reunited,
I shall smile at you as soon
As I finish crying.
But you won't have to act this way.
You can look at me with an upturned face—
Like a dew-drenched rose
At sunset on a clearing day—
And let the tears dry.

14

I am sending you these poems.
If you don't know all the words,
It doesn't matter.
You can use your fingers
To touch them gently,
Like a doctor feeling a patient's pulse.
Perhaps you can tell
They throb
To the rhythm of your heart.

23

We are two water reeds.
From the speed with which we part
And the distance that comes between us
We can measure how hard the wind blows,
How high the tides rise.

PERHAPS (A DIRGE)

Perhaps you have cried yourself tired;
Perhaps you feel like taking a nap.
Then I'll tell the owls not to cough,
The frogs not to croak, and the bats not to fly.

I won't let the sun pry your eyelids up
Or the wind brush your forehead.
No one will startle or awaken you;
A pine parasol will shade you.

Perhaps you will hear earthworms turning soil
And grass roots sucking water;
Perhaps the music you hear
Will be sweeter than human curses.

Then close your eyes tightly;
I'll let you sleep, let you sleep.
I'll cover you gently with yellow earth
And set the smoke of paper gold slowly rising.

CONFESSION

I am not lying to you: I'm not a poet,
Though I love steadfast gray rocks,
Green pines, the sea, the sunset on crows' backs,
And twilight woven with bats' wings.
You know I love heroes and mountains,
The national flag fluttering in the wind,
And chrysanthemums of pale yellow or dark bronze.
My staple food, remember, is a jug of bitter tea.

But there is another me—are you scared or not?—
With thoughts like flies crawling in the garbage can.

THE END

Dewdrops are sobbing in the hollows of bamboos,
    The green tongues of plantains are licking the windowpanes,
The four walls are receding—
    Alone, I cannot fill this empty room.

I build a fire in my heart
    And wait quietly for the guest from afar.
I stoke it with cobwebs and rat droppings
    And mottled snake scales.

Roosters hurry me when ashes lie in the fireplace.
    A cold wind sneaks up and touches my lips—
So the guest has arrived.
    Closing my eyes, I follow him out.

DEAD WATER

A bleak pool of dead water
Where no breeze can raise a ripple—
One may as well throw in metal scraps
And leftover food.

Perhaps the metal will turn into emeralds,
The rusty cans into peach blossoms;
The grease will weave a silken gauze,
And the mold will rise and become twilight clouds.

Let the dead water ferment into a green wine
In which white foam floats like pearls;
Tiny pearls giggle and turn into big pearls,
Then get broken by pilfering mosquitoes.

Perhaps a bleak pool of dead water
Is fair after all.
If the frogs get lonely,
They can bring music to the place.

A bleak pool of dead water
Where beauty cannot reside—
One may as well let the Devil cultivate it
And see what kind of world he will create.

Li Jinfa

(Li Chin-fa, 1900–1976)

A native of Guangdong, Li Shuliang was educated in Hong Kong, Shanghai, and France. All three volumes of his poetry were written and published between 1919 and 1925 while he was studying sculpture in France. He taught art when he returned to China in 1926, then, in 1932, turned to a career in diplomacy, serving the Nationalist government in Iran and Iraq. In 1951 he emigrated to the United States, where he lived in New Jersey until his death of a heart attack in December 1976.

Li adopted the pen name Jinfa (Golden Hair) after the blond goddess who appeared in his delirium when he was stricken ill in Paris in 1922. His acknowledged influences include such French Symbolists as Baudelaire, Verlaine, Rémy de Gourmont, and Rimbaud. Much of the notorious obscurity of his poetry comes from its dense imagery and the mixture of classical and modern diction.

WOMAN FORSAKEN

Long hair hangs before my eyes,
Blocking the shaming stares,
The rapid flow of fresh blood, the slumber of dry bones.
Dark night and insects come with the same footsteps
Over the low wall
And yelp into my chaste ears
Like the howling wind
That makes all the nomads shiver.

With a blade of grass, I traverse the empty vale with God;
My sorrow finds the register in a flitting bee's brain
Or hangs down the cliff with a mountain spring
And then disappears with red leaves.
The grief of a forsaken woman weighs on her movements;
The flame of the setting sun cannot turn her distress
Into smoke rising from the embers
Or dye the wings of a vagrant crow
And perch with it on a rock in a tumbling sea
To listen quietly to a mariner's song.

The decrepit skirt groans
And wanders by the graves.
No more scalding tears
To adorn the grasses
Of the world.

THOU MAYEST COME NAKED

Thou mayest come naked to the garden;
My roses are blooming.
They long to vie with thy beauty—
But loving eyes must be barred.

Thou mayest sleep dreamlessly
On the moist dark moss.
If thy legs get wet, I will
Dry them with refracted sunlight.

Thou mayest not heed the lure of pretty eyes
Because spring is gone, and
They are tracking it home;
Spring is not on the willow tips nor in the grassy pond.

Thou mayest clutch thy golden locks
So the west wind won't blow them
Into the travelers' arms
To compete in number with their dismal thoughts.

TENDERNESS

1

Your dazzling smiles come and go in the breeze;
They bloom at the tips of branches in my garden.
The grass reminds me of the skirt you loved;
It has grown pale in the faithful spring.

The past deludes us most;
It makes our hearts tremble
Yet never offers true solace,
Like the April breeze that blows away superficial grief.

Although nature chuckles with me,
I cannot peek into the river of fate.
Like a stream in springtime,
It vanishes into the desert of yellow sand.

Although together we can create God,
In the morning light I always regret our love.
Oh, your scent and your touch in the night
Have extinguished the flames of my life.

You come on tiptoe over mystery's threshold.
When will I be able to know
Your power, love, beauty, and skill,
Rippling forever by the willow-banked dam?

4

With my presumptuous fingertips
I feel the warmth of your skin—
A young doe has lost her way in the forest;
There is only the sound of dead leaves.

Your soft breathing
Calls out to my desolate heart.
Conqueror of all, I have
Smashed my shield and my spear.

The loving look in your eyes
Is like a butcher's sign for slaughter.
Your lips? No need to mention them—
I'd rather trust your arms.

I'd rather believe in fairy tales
Than in the love of a woman.
(I'm not good at comparison to begin with,
But you are indeed like the shepherdess in a romance.)

I have played all the tunes,
But none pleases your ears;
I have mixed all the colors,
But none can match your beauty.

1922

MISFORTUNE

The flowers of our souls are broken,
So we cry bitterly in a dark room.
The sun behind the mountain range cannot dry
Our tears; it dissipates just the dawn haze.
How ashamed I am. A nightingale is singing.
Bring me your lyre, and I'll tell it my sorrows
And ask it to spread the tale as it roams.

We interact with a stupid language.
Only your lyre can relate—
And only spring can understand—the fall of a soul.
Except for truth, we know no greater thing.
"Open your arms," the night is whispering.
A night owl has arrived, bringing us, I fear,
Endless sorrow.

Bing Xin

(Ping Hsin, b. 1900)

Xie Wanying, a native of Fujian, spent her childhood in coastal Shanghai and Yantai. As a student at Yanjing University (then Yanjing Women's University), she participated in the May Fourth Movement of 1919 and started writing short stories under the pen name Bing Xin, or "pure heart," in the same year. She published two volumes of short poems, *Myriad Stars* and *Springwater*, in 1923, which established her as a pioneer of modern Chinese poetry. After graduating in 1923, Bing Xin went to the United States and studied at Wellesley, receiving her M.A. in English in 1926. While abroad she wrote the famous twenty-nine "Letters to Young Readers," generally considered the earliest children's literature in modern China.

"Paper Boat—Sent to Mother" was written on her voyage from China to the United States in 1923.

MYRIAD STARS

131
O Sea,
  Which star is not bright?
  Which flower is not fragrant?
  Which thought of mine does not ring
    With the pure sound of your tides?

132
My heart,
Yesterday you told me
  The world is joyful,
Yet today you tell me
  The world is disappointing.
What will
  Your words be tomorrow?
How can I believe you!

SPRINGWATER

105

Creator,
  If in eternal life
  Only one wish is granted,
I will plead in all sincerity:
  "Let me be in my mother's arms,
    Let Mother be in a small boat,
    Let the small boat be on a moonlit sea."

Published in 1923

PAPER BOAT—SENT TO MOTHER

I never throw away a piece of paper.
  I always save it.
I fold it into a tiny boat
  And cast it into the sea.

Some boats blow into a porthole;
  Some get drenched by the waves and stick to the bow.
I still fold paper boats every day,
  Hoping that one will float where I wish it to.

Mother, if you see a little white boat in your dream,
  Do not think, startled, that it comes for no reason.
It was folded by your dearest daughter, with teary eyes,
  Who begged it to sail across the miles with her smile and her sorrow.

August 27, 1923

Fei Ming

(1901–67)

Fei Ming, who wrote short stories under his real name, Feng Wenbing, studied English literature at Beijing University in the early 1920s and taught Chinese literature at his alma mater after 1949.

  The first line in "A Pot of Flowers" quotes from the famous lines by Xie Lingyun: "Spring grass has sprouted in the pond; / Garden willows have turned into singing birds." The poem "To Zhilin" was written for a college friend, the poet Bian Zhilin; the line "A giant tree showering leaves" is quoted from Du Fu's (712–70) "Climbing the Heights."

Fei Ming

VANITY STAND

Because I dreamed I was a mirror
Sunk in the sea, I became a mirror.
A young woman picked it up
And put it on her vanity stand.
Because this is her vanity stand,
No sadness is allowed.

May 16, 1931

A POT OF FLOWERS

Spring grass has sprouted in the pond.
A tree by the pond
Says, "I used to be a seed."
The grass says, "We come from the same source."
The gardener comes along
And says to the tree,
"How tall my tree has grown.
I don't know where my grave will be,"
As if he wants to carry a pot of flowers inside his grave.

May 18, 1931

LITTLE GARDEN

I planted a flower in a corner of my small garden,
Where it grew to my heart's delight.
I wanted to send it to my love
And felt sad that I could not.
I could not even tell her the flower's name—
Could it be My Grave?

1931

SNOWFIELD

Snowfield,
You are an unborn child.
The moon doesn't know you,
Tomorrow's sun doesn't know you.
Do tonight's footprints belong to a beast?
The tree shadows don't know.
Snowfield,
You are an unborn child.
Is your soul the light in that house?
Lamp and fire do not know each other.
Snowfield,
You are an unborn child.
An unborn child
Is the soul of the universe—
A poem of snowy night.

THE NIGHT OF DECEMBER NINETEENTH

Late at night, a single lamp
Is like mountains and rivers
And a sea beyond them.
The starry sky is a forest of birds,
It is flowers, fish,
A dream in the sky.
The sea is the night's mirror,
Thought is beauty,
Home,
The sun,
The moon,
Light,
Fire in the fireplace.
Fire in the fireplace is tree shadows on the wall,
The sound of a winter night.

1936

STREET CORNER

I walked to the street corner
As a car drove by—
Thus, the loneliness of the mailbox,
Thus, no memory of license number X,*
Thus, the loneliness of the Arabic numbers,
The loneliness of the car,
The loneliness of the street,
The loneliness of humankind.

1937

TO ZHILIN

I said: "Let me write a letter to the poet in the south."
Then I spotted the scant shadow of a tree in the yard.
It had written a letter to noontime.
I felt like writing a poem
Like the sun, the moon,
The shade at noon,
A giant tree showering leaves—
My poem doesn't have even two leaves.

May 8, 1937

Zhu Xiang

(Chu Hsiang, 1904–33)

Zhu was born in Hunan. He started writing poetry in 1921 and joined
the Literary Research Society in 1922. He attended Qinghua University
but was expelled in 1923 owing to excessive absences; later he reenrolled
and graduated. In 1927–29 he studied Western literature at Lawrence
University (Wisconsin), the University of Chicago, and Ohio University
without receiving a degree. After returning to China in 1929, he became
chair of the English Department at Anhui University, a post he quit
three years later because of conflicts with the president. He drowned
himself while taking a steamboat from Shanghai to Nanjing.

*In English in the original: "P O" (for mailbox) and "X."

Zhu was briefly associated with the Crescent school; like Wen Yiduo, he emphasized poetic form and experimented with Western varieties like the ballad, rondeau, sonnet, and blank verse.

RAINSCAPE

Many are the rain sounds that I love—
The pitter-patter at my window when I awake on a spring night,
The swift drops beating on plantain leaves,
The drizzle brushing against my face,
The thundering rain pouring down in flashes of lightning—
But my favorite is the sky before the rain.
Though gray, it is translucent
And holds silent anticipation;
Then somewhere from the misty clouds
Comes the crisp twittering of a bird.

November 22, 1924

A BROOK

The sea is my mother,
Toward whose bosom I flow.
Someday
She will hold my tired body
And rock it in her arms
While she hums a lullaby.
My soul will turn into a cloud
That, drifting, rises in the sky,
Then, transformed, falls to earth—
Attracted by the sea's love.
In a heavy spring shower
A distant brook will come alive.

Published in 1925

Zhu Xiang

BURY ME

Bury me in a lily pond,
Where I'll hear worms crawling by.
On the lanterns of green leaves,
Fireflies switch off and on.

Bury me under the lantana blossoms,
Where I'll dream an eternal sweet dream.
Bury me on the top of Mount Tai,
Where the wind sobs in the lone pine—

Or burn me into ashes
And throw me into a churning spring river.
I'll flow with the fallen petals
To a place no one knows.

February 2, 1925

REPLY TO A DREAM

Why can't I put it behind me?
Because I am drifting on the sea.
Your love is like a bright star
Gazing at me from a clear sky—
    Lifting me from sinking despair,
    Making me strive with courage.

Why can't I put it behind me?
It is you who left me with love
In a dream when I was unaware
And staged a play like a mischievous boy—
    How I wish I could stay in that dream
    And always be with you.

Why can't I put it behind me?
We have no time to unclasp our hands.
Love is like expanding ripples;
Though they are contained by the banks,
    The willows by the lake, tremulous,
    Kiss the water with their branches.

Love's intensity grows in time
Like a mountain's beauty growing with distance.
The green palm shades seem lovelier
When the traveler has crossed desert sand—
    Love, please send your reply to me.
    How can I put her behind me?

May 19, 1925

PAWNSHOP

Beauty has opened a pawnshop
That specializes in hearts.
When the time comes for redemption,
It closes the shop.

October 15, 1925

HAPPINESS

    Happiness, never
Have I seen your face,
    Except in hard times, when
Those lighthearted days of the past bring a sweetness.
    Then you reveal your true self,
    Saying, "To be carefree is the highest happiness,"
And after that, vanishing in smoke.

    Sometimes I look at the sky
As I trudge toward the Star of Hope.
    On the way I amuse myself by
Allowing my deceitful fancy to conjure
    A bliss not belonging to this world.
    At journey's end there are only foul birds
In the wilderness laughing at me.

Why prolong this life even by an instant
If no happiness is stored for the years to come?
   Yet the future is an enigma;
What novelties does it hold?
   Who wouldn't like to see them?
   So, as long as I am discontent,
I will not close my eyes and sleep for good.

Published in 1930

SONNETS IN THE ITALIAN STYLE

19. Hawthorne
If only I could own that mossy cottage of yours,
Where I'd enjoy the greenery from the porch by day
And read by night, or with some friends
Listen to the dialogue between chestnuts and firewood;
If only I could have those keen eyes of yours,
Like Dante's, able to discern the tip of a wing,
A bee dying, a flower trembling in its nakedness,
A slender twig sprouting from decayed roots;

If only I could see life the way you do,
Admire the evening view yet know the spectacle
Is but a trick Apollo plays—
But only for a moment do insects hum like the sea;
Once the sound is gone, only misty clouds remain, or
Perhaps, a little better, a bright moon rising in the east.

Lin Huiyin

(Lin Hui-yin, 1904–55)

Born into a gentry family in Fujian Province, Lin grew up in Beijing and went to England with her father in 1920–21. She wanted to study architecture but majored in art because the School of Architecture at the University of Pennsylvania did not admit women; she received her B.A. in 1927. Lin married Liang Sicheng, later a famous architect. He was the son of Liang Qichao, the eminent statesman and a leading intellectual. After they returned to China, they devoted their lives to the study and teaching of traditional Chinese architecture. Lin died of a chronic lung disease.

Lin Huiyin

DO NOT THROW AWAY

Do not throw away
That scoop of passion from the past.
Even though passion flows softly like water
At the bottom of a cool mountain spring
In a pine grove on a dark night
And sighs an elusive sigh,
You must still preserve that truth.
The moon is still bright;
The lights below the hills are still on;
The sky is still full of stars
Hanging like dreams.
You ask the night for
Those words back—you must still believe
Their echoes
In the valley.

Summer 1932

MEDITATION

My heart at this moment is as quiet as a desert,
My thought as lonely as an Arab,
His face lifted, gazing at the sunset
At the end of the sky and listening
To the distant bells of a herd of returning camels.

In those white surroundings
Everything stands as still as sculpture—
His white robe, the dagger at his waist, his tall turban,
The wavelike clouds, the wind over the desert.
Once in a while a light flashes on the horizon—
A lone star in the fading twilight.

Summer 1936

SITTING IN QUIETUDE

Winter has a message of its own
When the cold is like a flower—
Flowers have their fragrance, winter has its handful of memories.
The shadow of a withered branch, like lean blue smoke,
Paints a stroke across the afternoon window.
In the cold the sunlight grows pale and slanted.
It is just like this.
I sip the tea quietly
As if waiting for a guest to speak.

November 1936

Dai Wangshu

(Tai Wang-shu, 1905–50)

Dai Wangshu is the pen name of Dai Meng'ou. A native of Zhejiang
Province, Dai studied at Shanghai University in 1923, joined the Com-
munist Youth Corps in 1925 and the League of Left-Wing Writers in
1931, then went to France in 1932. There he attended the University of
Lyons and later the University of Paris. After traveling in Spain, he re-
turned to China in 1935. In 1938 he moved to Hong Kong, where he was
the editor in chief of the literary supplements of several newspapers. For
his anti-Japanese activities, he was arrested and incarcerated for three
months in 1941–42. His health severely impaired, Dai continued to do
editorial work. After returning to the mainland in 1949, he was in charge
of translation in the French section of the International News Bureau
(later renamed Foreign Languages Press). He died of asthma complications.

One poem was written for Xiao Hong (1911–42), a writer, who lived
in Hong Kong for the last year of her life.

ALLEY IN THE RAIN

With an oil-paper umbrella, alone I
Wander in a long
Lonely alley in the rain,
Hoping to meet
A melancholy girl
Like a lilac.

She has
The coloring of a lilac,
The fragrance of a lilac,
The sorrow of a lilac—
Melancholy in the rain,
Melancholy and lost.

She wanders in the lonely alley in the rain
With an oil-paper umbrella
Like me,
Just like me,
Roaming quietly,
Indifferent, sad, and wistful.

She comes close
And casts
A look like a sigh;
She drifts by
Like a dream,
Like a sad, bewildering dream.

She drifts by like a lilac
In a dream;
The girl drifts by me.
She walks farther and farther
Until she reaches the broken fence
At the end of the alley in the rain.

Gone is her color,
Dimmed by the sad tune of the rain;
Gone is her fragrance;
Even her gaze like a sigh,
Her lilaclike wistfulness,
Are dispersed.

Alone, with an oil-paper umbrella I
Wander in this long
Lonely alley in the rain,
Hoping to meet
A melancholy girl
Like a lilac.

OUT OF SORTS

The scent of the earth seeps through the bamboo curtain
And congeals in the early spring wind.
I feel out of sorts, the crisp taste of lettuce in my mouth
Making me yearn for the garden back home.

There the sunlight lingers on the winter rape,
A breeze rests on the wings of slender-waisted bees,
A sick man eats the insect-bitten turnip leaves,
Chinese chives sprout after the rain.

These days I fear the delicacies that make my hair fall out;
I even have to give up the tasty eel.
For this ailing body is frail in the early spring breeze—
Besides, I crave the lettuce in the sun in my garden.

AUTUMN

In a few days autumn will be here.
While I sit quietly and smoke a pipe
I seem to hear it singing
In the sails on the river.

It plays a stringed instrument,
Reminding me of a dream I once had.
It has brought me nothing but sorrow,
Though I mistakenly thought it was a friend.

The sound of a hunting horn in the woods is pleasing;
So is walking on dead leaves.
But I know how a bachelor feels;
Today I am in no mood to take my ease.

I neither love nor fear autumn;
Well do I know the weight of its load.
Sitting by the window, I just smile
At the floating clouds that try to intimidate me:
    "Autumn is coming, Mr. Wangshu!"

Published in January 1929

Dai Wangshu

LONELINESS

Wild grass is growing thicker in the garden,
Taking root where my old footsteps fell.
It is now clad in the bright gown of youth.
My strolls under the stars have long since ceased.

Days go by, but loneliness remains.
Like those pitiful souls,
I entrusted my heart to the thick wild grass
Now as tall as I am.

I no longer go into the garden,
Where loneliness is as tall as I am.
At night I sit listening to the wind,
During the day I lie listening to the rain, and learn how the moon wanes
    and the heavens age.

February 12, 1937

I THINK

I think, therefore I am a butterfly.
Ten millennia from now, a tiny flower's gentle call—
Through clouds of no dreams and no awakenings—
Shall flutter my colorful wings.

March 14, 1937

MY MEMORY

My memory is loyal to me,
More loyal than my best friends.

It lives in a burning cigarette,
In a pen painted with a lily,
In an old powder compact,
In the berries on the shabby fence,
In a half-empty bottle,
In a torn manuscript, in dried flower petals,
In the gloomy lamp, in still water,
In all things with or without souls.
It lives everywhere, the way I do in this world.

It is timid; it fears human clamor.
But when I am lonely, it visits me.
Its voice is low,
Yet its speech is trivial
And goes on and on:
Old words repeating stories,
Harmony humming the same tune.
Sometimes it mimics a coquette
With a faint voice
Mixed with tears and sighs.

Its visits are unpredictable;
It comes anytime, anyplace,
Often when I'm in bed, drifting into sleep,
Or early in the morning.
People would call it rude,
But we are old friends.

It never stops talking
Unless I break into sobs
Or fall into a deep sleep.
But I will never tire of it,
Because it is loyal to me.

WITH MY MAIMED HAND

With my maimed hand
I feel the vast land:
This corner is reduced to ashes;
That corner is nothing but blood and mud.
This lake must be my hometown—
I can feel the coolness of the reeds by the water.
(In spring, flowers make a brocade screen on the bank;
Delicate willow twigs, breaking, scent the air.)
I touch the cool reeds and waters;
The snowcapped peaks of Changbai chill me to the bone.
The gritty water of the Yellow River slips through my fingers;
The rice paddies in the south—where young sprouts
Were so tender—now just have weeds,
and the litchi flowers languish in loneliness.

Farther south still, I dip in the bitter water of
The South China Sea, where no fishing boats sail.
My invisible hand travels across the vast land,
Its fingers stained with blood and mud, its palm dirty.
Only that distant corner is still whole—
Warm, bright, strong, and vital—
I caress it with my maimed hand
As if touching my love's soft hair or a sucking baby's fingers.
I concentrate all my strength in my hand
And press it there with all my love and hope,
For only there can we see the sunshine and the spring
That chase darkness away and bring new life;
For only there do we not live like stock animals
And die like ants—there, in our eternal China.

July 3, 1942

BY XIAO HONG'S TOMB, AN IMPROMPTU

A lonely walk of six hours
To lay red camellias by your head—
I wait through the night,
While you lie listening to the chitchat of the ocean tides.

November 20, 1944

IMPROMPTU

If the spring of life comes again
And ancient ice melts with a clink,
Then I shall once more see that radiant smile
And hear that ringing call—those distant dreams.

The good things will never disappear,
For all good things last forever;
They only freeze like ice,
One day to bloom again like flowers.

May 31, 1945

Feng Zhi

(Feng Chih, b. 1905)

Feng Zhi, born Feng Chengzhi, is from Hebei. He studied German at
Beijing University in 1922–27 and was a founding member of the Pale
Grass Club in Shanghai in 1923 and of the Sunken Bell Club in Beijing
in 1925. From October 1930 to June 1935 he studied in Berlin and Hei-
delberg, then returned to China, where he taught at various universities.
He is now director of the Research Institute of Foreign Literatures at the
Chinese Academy of Social Sciences and vice chair of the Chinese
Writers' League.

SNAKE

My loneliness is a snake,
Reticent, without a word.
If by chance you dream of it,
Please do not be alarmed.

It is my faithful companion,
Stricken with homesickness.
It misses that lush prairie—
The black silk on your head.

Like a moon shadow, it
Passes by you softly;
It takes your dream away in the mouth
Like a scarlet flower.

1926

SOUTHERN NIGHT

We sit by the edge of the lake
And listen to swallows singing about serene southern nights.
They have brought us a night from the south
When the reeds radiate a deep warmth—
    I am drunk with the night.
    Can you, too, smell the heavy scent of the reeds?

You say Ursa Major resembles a polar bear;
The sight chills you all over.

At this moment the swallows ballet across the water,
Ruffling the stars' reflections—
   Will you look at the stars in the lake?
   Just as starry is the southern night.

You say you suspect the white pines there
Are still clad in snow.
At this moment the swallows flit to the palms
And release a passionate song—
   Will you listen to the swallows singing?
   Such is the sound in the southern grove.

We feel that we don't belong in the tropics;
Our hearts hold the quietude of winter and fall.
The swallows say there is a rare flower in the south
That blooms every twenty lonely years—
   At this moment the flower hidden in my bosom
   Bursts forth like a flame in the night.

1929

SONNETS

1

We are prepared to experience
Unexpected miracles.
After long years a meteor
Or a gust of wind suddenly appears.

At such moments,
As in our first embrace,
All past joys and sorrows come before us
And congeal.

We praise those tiny insects
Who, after mating
Or warding off a threat,

Conclude their wondrous lives.
Our entire life is to endure
A gust of wind, the fall of a meteor.

2

That which our bodies shed—
Let it turn into ashes and dust.
These days we arrange ourselves
One by one, like trees in autumn.

Handing leaves and late blossoms
To the autumn wind, trunks stretching
Into deep winter, we arrange ourselves
In nature like moths metamorphosing,

Shedding their cocoons in the mud.
We arrange ourselves for
Death to come like a song,

Its melody falling off
Until only the body of music is left,
Turning into a range of silent blue hills.

6

In the fields I often see
A village boy or peasant woman
Wailing to the clear, wordless sky.
Is it over some punishment

Or a broken toy?
Is it because of a husband's death
Or a son's illness?
Crying like that, never stopping,

It is as if their whole life is laid
In a frame, and outside the frame
There is no life, no world.

I feel that since antiquity
They have been crying incessantly
Over a despairing universe.

16

Standing on top of the mountain,
We become the boundless view
In front of us: an immense prairie
With crisscross paths.

What paths, what streams, are not connected?
What winds, what clouds, do not answer each other?
The towns, mountains, and rivers that we've traversed
Have become part of our lives.

Our growth, our grief,
Is a pine tree on a mountain
Or the heavy fog over a city.

We blow in the wind, we flow with the waters,
We turn into the crisscross paths on the prairie,
Into the lives of the travelers on the paths.

19
With a wave of the hand, separation
Bisects our world.
We feel cold, the vista opens up;
We are like two newborns.

Ah, each separation, each birth:
We toil to turn coldness
Into warmth, rawness into ripeness.
We cultivate our own worlds

In order to meet again, as if for the first time.
We gratefully recall
How our previous lives flashed by when we first met.

How many springs and winters does one life have?
We experience the seasons
But not our human-reckoned years of age.

27
To the overflowing amorphous water
The water bearer brings a rounded jar;
From it the water receives a definite shape.
Look, the banner flutters in the autumn wind.

It holds that which cannot be held.
Let the distant light, the dark, distant night,
The glory and decay of plants and trees,
And the heart striving for the infinite

Be preserved on the banner in the wind.
In vain have we listened to the night wind;
In vain have we looked at yellow grass and red leaves during the day.

Where are we to arrange our thoughts?
May these poems be a banner in the wind,
Holding some of that which cannot be held.

1941

Luo Dagang

(Lo Ta-gang, b. 1909)

Luo, who was born in Zhejiang, majored in French at the Sino-French
University in Beijing and lived in France and other parts of Europe for
fourteen years (1933–47). He currently teaches at Beijing University
and is a research fellow at the Research Institute of Foreign Literatures
at the Chinese Academy of Social Sciences. He has published poems in
both Chinese and French.

The floating world in the eighth verse in "Homesickness" refers to the
ephemeral world of human desire. Buddhism advocates renunciation of
this world. The shed in the ninth verse has a bamboo framework and
mat sides. It is customary to set up such sheds in the spring and
dismantle them in the fall.

A SHORT VERSE FOR S.

Even night birds
Lose their way in broad daylight.
With the fog as thick as a dream
Here I am, writing these words to you.

Here I am, writing these words to you
As if you did not exist.

I call out to you silently.
The look in your eyes swims
In the palm of my hand.

Your name
Is so tiny,
Circling gently in my call

Like a bee in a hive,
Like your arm
Encircling mine.

I know you are by my side.
I know you are not.
So close,
Yet so far.

A light rain sprinkles down.
Here I am, writing these words to you—
Are your eyes moist?

I ask my fingers,
My hair,
If they might be your fingers,
Your hair.

But with cat feet
You tiptoe on my nerves.
I may as well let the skiff capsize,
Let the dragonflies be silhouetted against the water.

Your shadow is sewed to mine.
Moonlight seeps through moonlight,
Like our breathing,
Like a concurrence of air.

Here I am, writing these words to you
As if you did not exist.

Here I am, writing these words to you.
They will say I didn't write them.
Let them say what they will.

HOMESICKNESS

1

In a dreamless dream, does the dream
Know the distance of the journey?
That which falls beyond the grove
Is but a shooting star.

2

When we are homesick,
We envy the fish swimming in water.
In the eyes of the blind, the night
Blossoms with a myriad flowers.

3

The small courtyard I have not visited for twenty years
Is covered with thick green moss in my dream.
I am about to search for the names you and I carved;
The wind-tossed leaves shower me with cold rain.

4

Wind and rain are incessant in the shrubs;
I am a spider weaving a web in the rain.
Why is memory as stubborn as a snake
Squirming about on the fallen leaves, refusing to freeze?

5

Walking in the rain makes you forget the distance;
The rain hums an eternal emerald melody. No umbrellas, please!
They disrupt the rhythm of the rain and cannot hide grief anyway;
If your face is covered, raindrops seep into your heart just the same.

6

Fortunately night buries fallen flowers in the dark;
No one pays attention to how many eyes are crying or smiling.
And you, every time you feel like laughing or crying,
Why only nod and say yes?

7

Please do not touch my face with your hairy hand.
Night, I know the multiple chambers of your heart.
Let me carry your grace alone, like a camel with a heavy load,
For fear that someone far away aches with my absence.

8

Old spring has returned on the back of a skinny dog,
Leaving behind the parched summer, cool autumn, and merciless winter.
What's there to keep me from renouncing this floating world?
In ten years or a hundred years there is nothing but the seasons, nothing
  but fallen flowers.

9

When fall comes, the shed in the yard is the first to succumb;
For nights on end, rain drips down the ropes.
The workers nimbly climb up to dismantle it;
Now only a skeleton holds up the blue sky.

10

During the day I press my ear to the radio in vain.
At night, how do I imagine long waves and short waves?
How do thirty-three heavens, the seas, and the clouds
Verify the mizzle at our arrival and the sandstorm when we depart?

11

The sea did not erase its thoughts intentionally;
Just read the crisscross tracks on the sand.
The old pearlless clam may hold the truth of the sea,
But only the tides know its secret love a thousand miles away.

12

A thousand miles away, at the other end of the sky,
A white cloud drifts in a traveler's dream night after night.
A lone sail is on the empty sea;
Tear-stained handkerchiefs still wave good-bye.

Ai Qing

(Ai Ch'ing, b. 1910)

Ai Qing is the pen name of Jiang Haicheng. A native of Zhejiang, Ai studied painting at the West Lake National Institute of Art in 1928 and left for France the following year. In January 1932 he returned to China, where he joined the Leftist Artists' League in Shanghai, only to be arrested in July. After his release in October 1935, he worked as an editor and teacher. He went to Yan'an in 1941 and joined the Communist Party in 1945. After 1949 he was assistant editor in chief of the journal *People's Literature.* He was persecuted during the Anti-Rightist Campaign of 1957–58 and the Cultural Revolution of 1966–76 and was rehabilitated in 1978.

GAMBLING MEN

At the shady bottom of the city wall,
In the dark corner by the houses,
Gamblers squat in the middle of a crowd,
Anxiously awaiting the outcome of a throw.

Filthy, ragged, stupid—yet inflamed—
Their bodies tremble, their heads squirm.
Cheers and curses
Accompany the clink of coins.

Women and children with disheveled hair
Goggle at them;
A hungry child kicks and wails,
But the mother is entranced by her husband's game.

They squat, stand up,
Slap their thighs and cry out in surprise.
Their faces are flushed, their mouths open,
As they try to reverse their fate in one throw.

They lose, then win, win, then lose again;
What stay the same are filth, poverty, and stupidity.
At nightfall they scatter, disappointed,
Returning to their dingy houses one by one.

SNOW IS FALLING ON THE LAND OF CHINA

Snow is falling on the land of China;
Coldness is blockading China.

Wind,
Like a grief-stricken old woman,
Trails closely behind,
Reaching out its frozen fingers,
Clutching the clothes of passers-by,
Muttering incessantly
Words as ancient as the land.

Emerging from the grove,
Driving a carriage,
You—a Chinese farmer

Wearing a fur hat—
Where are you going
In this heavy snow?

Let me tell you,
I, too, am a descendent of farmers.
Because of your
Pain-wrinkled faces,
I am deeply
Aware of
The plight of prairie dwellers.

As for me,
I am no happier than you are,
Lying in the river of time.
Waves of suffering
Have swallowed me and tossed me up repeatedly;
Drifting and incarceration
Have cost me the most precious days
Of my youth.
My life
Is as gaunt
As yours.

Snow is falling on the land of China;
Cold is blockading China.

Along the river on a snowy night,
Someone carrying an oil lamp staggers on.
Someone in the shabby black-topped boat
Sits by a lamp, head down—
Who is that person?

Oh, you
Disheveled young wife,
Is it true that
Your home—
That warm, happy nest—
Was burned down
By atrocious enemies?
Was it on
A night like this
That, without your man's protection

Against the terror of death,
You were ravished by enemy bayonets?

Alas, it is on a night this cold
That many of
Our aged mothers
Are crouching in places away from home,
Strangers,
Not knowing what road
The wheels will roll on tomorrow.
Besides,
The roads of China
Are tortuous
And muddy.

Snow is falling on the land of China;
Cold is blockading China.

Across the prairie on a snowy night,
In land gnawed by beacon fires,
Many a tiller of soil
Has lost his stock
And his fertile fields
And is living in despair,
Crammed in a filthy alley:
The famished earth
Stretches out its trembling
Beseeching arms
Toward the darkened sky.
The trials and tribulations of China
Are as immense and long as this snowy night.

Snow is falling on the land of China;
Coldness is blockading China.

China,
These impotent lines I have written
On a lightless night—
Can they give you a little warmth?

December 28, 1937

A YOUNG MAN'S VOYAGE

Like a fragrant canoe
Leaving a deserted island,
A passionate yet sad youth
Is leaving his village.

I dislike that village—
It is as common as a banyan tree,
As dumb as a water buffalo.
I spent my childhood there.

Those stupider than I laughed at me;
I kept silent but cherished a wish in my heart:
To go to the outside world to learn more,
To go far away—to places unseen even in dreams.

There will be far better than here.
People live like immortals;
They do not hear the heartbreaking sound of mortars
Or see the deplorable faces of monks and nuns.

Father counted out five gold coins,
Wrapped them in red paper, and lectured me.
But all the while I was thinking of something else,
Of that seaport dazzling in the light.

What are you garrulous swallows chirping about?
Don't you know that I am leaving?
And you simplehearted tenant farmers,
Why do you always wear grief on your faces?

The early morning sun shines on the cobbled road.
I feel sorry for the village:
Like a weak old man,
It stands under twin mountain peaks.

Farewell, my poor village.
Go back, my old dog.
May the twin peaks keep you safe and healthy.
When I am old, I will come back to be with you.

Bian Zhilin

(Pien Chih-lin, b. 1910)

A native of Jiangsu, Bian majored in English at Beijing University in 1929–33. He started writing poetry in 1927 and published a volume of poetry, *The Han Garden,* with his friends He Qifang and Li Guangtian (1906–68). Since the late 1930s, he has taught at various universities, including the Lu Xun Institute of Art and Literature; Southwest United, Nankai, and Beijing universities; and, from 1947 to 1949, Oxford University. Currently, he is a research fellow at the Chinese Academy of Social Sciences.

Bian is an accomplished translator of such diverse writers as Shakespeare, T. S. Eliot, W. H. Auden, Baudelaire, Paul Verlaine, André Gide, and Azorín (pen name of José Martínez Ruiz).

"Dream of an Old Town" features a fortune-teller, also called the blind man; besides fortune-telling, the pursuits of blind people in China traditionally included music playing, cricket selling, and massage. According to an old superstition, babies who cry excessively are being disturbed by evil spirits, hence the suggestion that the counsel of a fortune-teller be solicited. In a footnote to the poem, Bian says the name of another character, Little Mao's Dad, was taken from a short story by Fei Ming; parents are commonly addressed as So-and-So's father or mother.

In "The Organization of Distances," the expression "I can't read soil under a lamp" refers to the news report about a man named Wang Tongchun who could tell where he was by looking at the soil under his feet. The query "Did someone play with my boat in the tub?" alludes to a story in *Strange Tales from the Liao Studio* in which a Daoist master, about to take a voyage, instructed his disciple not to open the lid of the tub while he was away. The curious disciple disobeyed and saw a tiny reed boat in the tub. He touched it with a finger, capsized it, and quickly turned it right side up, then put the lid back on the tub. When the master came back, he scolded the disciple for nearly drowning him.

In "Untitled 4," the mud is carried to the eaves by swallows building nests.

DREAM OF AN OLD TOWN

There are two sounds in the small town,
Equally lonely:
During the day it's the fortune-teller's gong,
At night it's the watchman's wooden clappers.

Unable to wake others from their dreams,
The blind man walks the streets
One step after another
As if dreaming himself.
He knows which cobblestones are low,
Which are high,
Which girl in which family is how old.

Sending others deeper into dreams,
The night watchman walks the streets,
One step after another,
As if dreaming himself.
He knows which cobblestones are low,
Which are high,
Which household has its door shut tight.

"It's the third watch of the night. Listen,
Little Mao's Dad.
The baby keeps us awake with his crying.
He cries so much when he dreams—
Let's find a fortune-teller tomorrow."

It is late at night;
It is a quiet afternoon.
He who claps the clappers is crossing the bridge;
He who beats the gong is crossing the bridge.
Ceaseless is the flowing water below.

August 11, 1933

AUTUMN WINDOW

Like a middle-aged man
Turning to see the footprints of the past—
Each step a desert—
He wakes up from confused dreams
And hears the evening crows across half the sky.

Watching the setting sun on the gray wall,
He thinks of a tuberculosis patient
In front of the ancient mirror of twilight
Dreaming of his ruddy youth.

October 26, 1933

ENTERING THE DREAM

Imagine yourself slightly ill
(On an autumn afternoon),
Looking at the gray sky and the sparse tree shadows on the
   windowpanes,
Lying on a pillow left by someone who has traveled far,
And thinking of the blurry lakes and hills, barely recognizable on the
   pillow,
As if they were the elusive trail of an old friend who has vanished in the
   wind,
As if they were things of the past written on faded stationery—
Traces of history visible under a lamp
In a book, yellowed with age, in front of an old man.
Will you not be lost
In the dream?

November 12, 1933

FRAGMENT

You are standing on a bridge enjoying the view;
Someone's watching you from a balcony.

The moon adorns your window;
You adorn someone else's dream.

August 1934

THE ORGANIZATION OF DISTANCES

I feel like going to a tower to read *Decline of the Roman Empire*
When I read the news of a meteor foretelling Rome's demise.
The paper drops. The map spreads out. I recall the words of a faraway
   friend.

The landscape on the postcard he sent me is growing dusky, too.
(Waking up at nightfall, I am bored. I'll go visit a friend.)
Gray skies, gray sea, gray roads—
Where am I? I can't read soil by lamplight.
All of a sudden, I hear my name a thousand doors away.
How tired I am! Did someone play with my boat in the tub?
My friend has brought snow—and five o'clock.

January 9, 1935

LONELINESS

Scared of loneliness,
A country boy kept a cricket by his pillow.
When he grew up and worked in town,
He bought a watch with a luminous face.

When little, he was envious of
The grass on a tomb—it was a home for crickets.
Now he has been dead for three hours;
His watch keeps on ticking.

October 26, 1935

MIGRATORY BIRDS

How many courtyards, how many squares of blue sky?
Divide them among yourselves, for I am leaving.
Let a belled white pigeon circle three times overhead—
But camel bells are far away. Listen.
I throw a yo-yo to keep you, fly a kite to bind you,
Send a paper eagle, a paper swallow, and a paper rooster
To the sky—to greet the wild geese from the south?
Am I a toy for some child?
I think I'll go to the library to check out *A Study of Migratory Birds*.
Tell me, are you for or against the new law
Forbidding airplanes to fly across the city sky?
My thoughts are like gossamers for little spiders:
They tie me to let me float. I am leaving.

I'll give it some thought at some other place.
How many courtyards, how many squares of blue sky?
How can I go on being an antenna,
Stretching out two arms on the roof in vain,
Never receiving the sound waves I desire?

March 1937

UNTITLED 4

Mud from across the river is carried to your eaves;
Springwater from across the courtyard is fetched to your cup;
Luxuries from across the sea adorn your breast—
I want to study trade history.

I paid a sigh last night
And received two smiles this morning,
Paid a flower in the mirror and received a moon in the water—
I'll keep a book of running accounts for you.

April 1937

TRAIN STATION

"Pull it out, pull it out"—from the depth of my dream
Another night train comes. This is reality.
Ancients by the river sigh over the tides;
I am standing at the train station like an advertisement.
Boy, listen to the bee fretting inside the window,
Nail a live butterfly to the wall
To decorate my reality here.
The old mattresses that once squeaked,
The small earthquakes that once shook my dreams,
My pounding heartbeats—
Do they now bewilder the train?
When did I ever want to be a station of dreams!

April 1937

WATER CONTENT

The sponge containing the most water
Is what I most admired in childhood.
Curiosity bathed in each and every chamber,
And I remember the delight of holding water.

Then I became concerned about travelers:
Water jar, please let the camels drink some more.
May you spongelike rain clouds
Come again and follow their dusty track.

Clouds are in the sky, ripe fruit on the tree.
Let cool rain fall on whoever reaches for the fruit above.
Who will squeeze a drop of lemon before
Tasting my sweet yet tasteless black tea?

I toast you. With wine? Maybe.
Last night I dreamed about water.
Don't say water is soft, Flowering Branch.
Lift up your sad face, lift it up.

May 1937

Lin Geng

(b. 1910)

A native of Beijing, Lin enrolled in Qinghua University in 1928, where he changed majors from physics to Chinese literature. He is a professor of Chinese literature at Beijing University.

The following poems all come from his first collection, *Night,* published in 1933.

TWILIGHT

Often I hear the footsteps of a child running toward me
And stopping abruptly in an instant of loneliness
Spring is a dark, clear pool of water
Reflecting everything

In the hazy twilight
On the road shaded by two rows of green trees
Is an unknown hope flying?
Yes, a black dragonfly
Dashes into the dark grass.

NIGHT

Night walks into the land of loneliness
Thus, tears are like wine

The primitive men made a fire
That burned fiercely in a forest
Were they whispering?

Outside the wall the hurried pitter-patter of hoofs
Retreats farther and farther—
A swift horse
I sing a song of blessing

MAY

If there were only one encounter in spring
How reluctant would we be to lose it?
Why do we sometimes
Try to catch a butterfly on the wing?
It has only one life

A reed pipe tune fills the hills and the village
It signals the arrival of spring
Is it not beautiful? On an evening like this
Those who sold their youth to hope
Are disappointed because of their youth

Happiness is this moment
When I awake to find the sky as clear as water
It reminds me of your eyes

When you say I am thinner, my heart
Falls gently beyond the sky

For one used to the sound of rifle shots
A long life must seem absurd
Isn't that so?
Cuckoos in May, a deer bleats in the wilderness.

Qin Zihao

(Ch'in Tzu-hao, 1912–63)

A native of Sichuan, Qin attended the Sino-French University in Beijing.
In 1935 he went to Japan and studied law. When the Sino-Japanese War
broke out in 1937, he returned to China to join the army as a reporter.
He later moved to Taiwan, where, in 1954, he founded the Blue Star
Poetry Club and the *Blue Star Poetry Journal* with Zhong Dingwen
(b. 1914), Deng Yuping (1925–85), Yu Guangzhong, and others.
Countering the Western leanings of the Modernist school in the 1950s
and 1960s, the *Blue Star Poetry Journal,* which is still in publication,
championed lyricism based on traditional Chinese poetry. Qin died of
cancer in 1963.

   The Bridge of Black Hair in the poem with that name is in east
Taiwan, on the route between Taidong and Xin'gang.

SEEDS OF POETRY

Will locks itself in a tiny room
An immense world in the room

A song of the century drifts by the ears
A roaring flame burns in the chest

It projects ideals onto blank paper
Sowing seeds of fire in the squares

Seeds of fire are a skyful of stars
All falling on the dark earth

When seeds of fire light up human hearts
It bids a smiling farewell to the world

COMPOSITION

Images superimposed upon images
Rhythms interwoven with rhythms
   Together they compose
      An Olympic playing field
      A round music hall

    Doves fly up from the center of clamor
Marathon runners race toward the distant tracks
Swimmers, poised like flying fish, plunge into the azure sea of the sky
High jumpers bounce to the arch of the rainbow
Whistles on the doves' backs are blowing,
    Playing in trills
  A tune too elusive to be heard

The tune comes from twilight on an islet
  There, falling rain like a curtain
    Fog like a drape
Through my many-pupiled eyes I see your charm
  In strangers' faces
Innumerable associations let me
  Compose your eyes and brows
Yet the round hall is quiet
  Like a convent cemetery with somber tombstones
I am used to listening to the sisters' soft footsteps
  Under the misty moonlight
They remind me of a stranger
      Walking into an art gallery

  A seed sprouts in your eyes
  A tree grows in my body secretly
The doomed moment makes the stars stop their revolutions
  Years are no more
  Seasons are no more
No more shall we see sunset paint the statue of the goddess rosy
  No more shall we see fruit fall in the forbidden garden
Climbing ivy caresses the corridor pillars with its soft, slender fingers
  Bach sighs incessantly on the G string of the violin
  I weep in the aura of your portrait

Dream and reality—can they never sustain each other?
   Only at the intersection of warp and woof
   At the tip of an eternally snow-capped peak
There life and dream are both frozen
   Do you know how I give
   And how I receive?

Images superimposed on images
Dreams layered on dreams
   Together they compose
        A convent full of murmuring
        An art gallery of meditations

BEYOND THE BORDER

The scenery beyond the border is displayed
Beyond city, beyond land, beyond sea
Beyond rainbow, beyond clouds, beyond blue sky
Beyond human vision
Vision beyond vision
Vision of the man beyond the border

The man beyond the border is a rover
He came from beyond the border
But he often roams on the horizon
Although there is not a single tree or blade of grass
He always enjoys the scenery beyond the border

CLOUD COTTAGE

Pines all over the mountain, sheep all over the mountain
An expanse of green, an expanse of white
By way of the shaded stone steps covered with green moss
I enter the garden from under the pine branches
With no key, I open
The door locked securely by the clouds

A tree of clouds reminds me of an island in a painting
And those marvelous trees on that island
Like flower lanterns kindled by the sun
With their candlewicks sparkling

We once imagined strolling under the trees
On a brightly lit path

Here the pine grove is like a green tent
Within it is a stone cottage
With pinecones everywhere like wind chimes
But they are mute, casting the stars' shadows on the walls
Waves of clouds pound on the windows
Like rolling tides without clamor

Windy days are music festivals
With round sticks, frisky pinecones
Play on the xylophone of clay roof tiles
Composing a symphony with the wind in the pines
As if you came to me from the island in the painting
Each step falls on a pine seed
Each step hits a musical note
Your footfalls are mysterious echoes

Pines all over the mountain, sheep all over the mountain
The lovers' world of green and white
Love's secret nests in the cottage
When we greet each other with our eyes
The stone cottage grows wings of clouds

CROSSING THE BRIDGE OF BLACK HAIR

A knife at his waist, an aborigine crosses the Bridge of Black Hair
Sea wind ruffles his long black hair
Glistening
Like a bat swooping into the sunset

The black-haired aborigine has returned
Flying white-crested egrets fill the sky
A pure white feather falls
A strand of my white hair
Melts into the old bronze-colored mirror
And dusk is a barber on the bridge
Setting my black hair on fire

A strand of my white hair
Melts into the old bronze-colored mirror
And I walk alone
In the empty land between the mountain and the sea

The harbor lies beyond the mountain
Spring is tied to the forest of black hair
When the bat turns blind
Boats loaded with love will float by
In the sea at dawn

He Qifang

(Ho Ch'i-fang, 1912–77)

A native of Sichuan, He studied philosophy at Beijing University from
1931 to 1935. His first works were published in 1929, and he came to
be known for both his poetry and his lyrical prose. In the summer of
1938 he went to Yan'an, taught at Lu Xun Institute of Art and Litera-
ture, and joined the Communist Party. After 1949 he held a number of
important positions, including director of the Literary Research Institute
at the Chinese Academy of Social Sciences and editor in chief of *Literary
Review.* He acknowledged being influenced by French Symbolist poetry
and Late Tang poetry in his early work.

Chengdu, the subject of a long poem, is the capital of Sichuan. During
the Sino-Japanese War (1937–45), the Nationalist government retreated
to the southwest province and declared Chongqing, a neighboring city,
the temporary capital of China. The war started in China on July 7,
1937, when the Japanese army opened fire at Marco Polo Bridge.

The author of the epigraph to the poem, Vasilii Iakovlevich Eroshenko
(1889–1952), was a Russian poet and writer of fairy tales. He lost his
eyesight to measles at the age of four. In 1921–23 he taught in China
and became acquainted with Lu Xun and others. After he returned to
Russia in 1923, he dedicated himself to translation and to the education
of the blind. Vladimir Mayakovsky (1883–1930) and Sergei Aleksandro-
vich Esenin (1895–1925), who are mentioned in "Chengdu," were also
Russian poets; both committed suicide.

PROPHECY

This heart-pounding day has finally arrived.
Ah, your approaching footfalls sigh like the night;
I can tell they are not whispering leaves and the night wind
Or the hoofs of deer galloping along the mossy paths.
Tell me, in your voice like silver bells,
Are you the youthful god of the prophecy?

You must come from the warm south.
Tell me about the moonlight and sunlight there.
Tell me how spring breezes make flowers bloom,
How swallows are enamored of green poplars.
I shall sleep with your dreamlike singing in my ears, my eyes closed:
I remember its warmth but have forgotten it, too.

Please stop here, stop your long, hard journey.
Come in, here is a tiger skin for you to sit on.
Let me burn the fallen leaves I have gathered;
Listen to me sing.
I shall sing high and low like the flame,
Like the flame, relating the lives of fallen leaves.

Do not go on. Ahead is the unending forest;
Ancient trees with the marks and patterns of beasts
Are entwined with pythons in a deathlike slumber—
Not a star can shine through the dense foliage.
You will hesitate to lay your second foot down
After hearing the hollow echo of the first.

Must you go? Please wait for me.
My feet know every safe path;
I shall sing an endless song to chase fatigue away
And, what's more, offer you the warmth of my hand.
When the deep darkness of the night blocks our sight,
You can gaze into my eyes.

You are not listening to my passionate song;
Your feet are not pausing despite my trembling.
Like a solemn breeze at twilight,
Gone are your proud footfalls.
Have you come and gone without a word after all?
Gone without a word, my youthful god?

Fall 1931

SHRINE TO THE EARTH GOD

Sunlight shines on the broad leaves of castor-oil plants,
Beehives nestle in the earth-god shrine.
Running against my shadow,
I have returned circuitously
And realized the stillness of time.

But on the grass,
Where are those short-armed children who chased after chirping crickets?
Where are those joyous cries of my childhood playmates,
Rising to the blue sky at the treetops?
The vast kingdom of childhood
Appears pathetically small
Under my feet, which are dusty with foreign dust.

In the desert, travelers treasure a glass of water;
A sailor resents the white waves beyond his oars.
I used to think I possessed a paradise
And hid it in the darkest corner of my memory.
Since then I have experienced the loneliness of an adult
And grown fonder of the mazes of paths in dreams.

1933

SANDSTORM DAYS

Imagine, at this moment
Dark waves are churning in the lake,
Wind is slashing across gray-tiled and
Yellow-tiled roofs,
Dust is twirling on the main street
Like wheels. Far away, in the suburbs,
An old-fashioned mule carriage stops
Midway, no household in the overgrowth around it.

The four walls make me lonesome.
Today the walls are even thicker,
With layers of wind-blown sand.

"Tonight the tide-loud north wind
Is rocking our cottage
Like a boat. My lonely companion,

Are you tired of this long journey?
We are on our way to the tropics;
There we shall turn into plants:
I will be an evergreen vine,
And you will be a tall bodhi tree."

At dusk I turn on
The lamp and open my book—
Open my memory like a brocade box.

March 31, 1934

AUTUMN

Shaking down the dew of early morning,
A clinking, lumbering sound drifts beyond the deep ravine.
The scythe, sated with scented rice, is laid down;
Shoulder baskets hold plump melons and fruits from the hedges.
Autumn is resting in a farmer's home.

A round net is cast into the river of cold mist
And collects the shadows of dark cypress leaves, like blue
Hoary frost on the tips of the reeds,
While homeward oars dip and pull.
Autumn is playing in the fishing boat.

The grassy field seems wider when the crickets chirp;
The stream looks clearer when it dries up.
Where did the bamboo flute on the ox's back go,
Its holes overflowing with summery scent and warmth?
Autumn is dreaming in the shepherdess's eyes.

CHENGDU, LET ME WAKE YOU GENTLY

There is indeed a big, glamorous Beijing, but my Beijing is small and quiet.
—V. I. Eroshenko

1
Chengdu is bleak and small,
Like a man
Falling asleep
After many profligate nights.

Although torches of protest have been burned,
Although sirens have pierced the ears,
Although shiploads of children
Have come to Chongqing from all the war areas
With only the country left as their parent,
Although night and day the enemies bomb
Guangzhou, our only port to the sea,
Although the new Great Wall, winding for miles,
Is built of the flesh and blood of frontline soldiers,
I cannot help sighing sadly
Like Eroshenko:
Although Chengdu is asleep,
It is not a place fit for sleeping.
This is not an age fit for sleeping.
This age makes me want to laugh loudly
And shout.
Yet Chengdu makes me lonely,
So lonely that I think of Mayakovsky's reproach
To Esenin for committing suicide:
"It is easier to die,
 Harder to live."

2

I used to sing in the north:

"Northland, bandits' fists have hit the nerves
 Of your arms, which have been paralyzed for years.
 Aren't you going to give them a few hard slaps?

"Northland, I am leaving you and going home
 Because there is little joy
 On your hardened prairies,
 And winter is so long."

Thus the cannons fired at Marco Polo Bridge.
The paralyzed arm
Is raised to flourish the battle flag.
Thus the enemies have taken our Beijing, Shanghai, Nanjing;
Numerous cities groan under their ravishment.
Thus everyone has forgotten individual joy and sorrow;
All the people in the country have formed a steel chain.

In this long steel chain
I am an exceedingly tiny link,
Yet I am as tough as the toughest.
Like a blind man opening his eyes at last,
I see light in the depth of the darkness,
A gigantic light,
Advancing
Toward me,
Toward my country.

3
But I am in Chengdu.
Here luxury and indolence are everywhere;
People indulge in gourmet food as in the last years of the Roman
  Empire.
Because filth, decay, and sin have
Filled its putrid stomach,
It lies asleep even on a sunny morning

Although torches of protest have been burned,
Although sirens have pierced the ears.

Let me open your windows, your doors.
Chengdu, let me wake you gently
On a sunny morning.

June 1938

I'D LIKE TO TALK ABOUT ALL
KINDS OF PURE THINGS

I'd like to talk about all kinds of pure things;
I'm thinking of my earliest friends, my earliest love.

Flowers on earth, stars in the sky,
People—all have hearts.
Nothing stays firm forever;
As the seasons turn, everything vanishes like morning dew.
But things that once shone are precious;
They won eternity with their brilliance.
With my earliest friends I read books, sitting on the grass;
We walked under the stars and talked about our future.
For poor children, those things were riches.

I once loved a girl quietly;
I enjoyed doing little things for her
Without a response from her or even her knowledge.
But my love was as full as the moon on the fifteenth of the month.
Ah, the dust of time has clouded my heart.
For too long I have not thought of them:
My earliest friends have long been sleeping in their graves,
My earliest love has long been a mother.
I am no longer a young man,
Nor have the seasons stopped turning;
There is still youth everywhere,
There are still open minds everywhere.
Young friends, let us go to the wilderness.
Under the soft blue sky
I'd like to talk to you about all kinds of pure things.

March 13, 1942

CLOUDS

"I love the clouds, the drifting clouds . . . "
I thought I was the man in Baudelaire's prose poem
Who stretched out his neck to gaze gloomily at the sky.

I went to the countryside.
Farmers had lost their land because of their honesty.
Their homes were reduced to the size of a farm implement.
During the day they looked for odd jobs in the fields,
At night they slept on the dry stone bridge.

I walked to the city by the sea.
On the asphalt street of winter,
Row after row of villas stood
Like prostitutes on a street corner,
Waiting for the laughter of summer
And the lust of potbellied merchants.

From now on I will argue loudly:

I'd rather have a thatched roof.
I don't love the clouds or the moon
Or the stars.

Xin Di

(Hsin Ti, b. 1912)

A native of Tianjin, Wang Xingdi, whose pen name is Xin Di, graduated
with a B.A. in English from Qinghua University in 1935. From 1936 to
1939, he studied English literature at Edinburgh University, where he
became acquainted with T. S. Eliot. In the 1940s he was a member of
the Nine Leaves, a circle of poets named after the volume of poems (not
published until 1981) by himself, Du Yunxie (b. 1918), Yuan Kejia (b.
1921), Hang Yuehe (b. 1917), Tang Qi (b. 1920), Tang Ti (b. 1920),
Chen Jingrong, Zheng Min, and Mu Dan. He is now a member of the
executive board of the Chinese Writers' League.

LIFE

At moments of solitude
I awake crying for no reason
But without tears.
Night after night an endless dream
Leaves a circle forever incomplete.
They say
The rustling outside the window
Comes from the night dew.
But life has taught me to believe
It is spring grass growing.

July 1934

SAILING

The sails are hoisted
To take us toward the setting sun
Brightness and age
Where the wind-blown sails kiss the dark water
Like black and white butterflies.

A bright moon above
A blue snake
Sports a luminous silver pearl
Voices from the mast

Carried by the wind—
Sailors inquiring about the rain and the stars.

From day to night
From night to day
We cannot sail beyond the circle
A circle ahead
A circle behind
An eternal
Boundless circle.

Unload the mists of life
Into the mist and water.

August 1934

FEBRUARY

"H.T., are you fond of your home?
Flowers next door are climbing over the wall."
But I love even more the latecoming spring in the north;
I love looking at the tipsy moon
In the high wind.
You know,
When a light carriage rolls over willow withes,
I shall be the driver,
Carrying off my, perhaps your,
Cape of wind, cape of rain.
"Yes, my friend, February rain is as fine as silk threads—
Fair weather of February."

February 1936

AUTUMN AFTERNOON

Sunlight spreads out like a bolt of silk;
A distant river, cold and white, is reflected on the glass pane.
How much coldness is sucked
Into the tiny feet of insects?
The gradual fading of time . . .

August 1936

OCTOBER SONG

Listen to the singing from afar.
The tongs tap by the fire,
The heart tonight, the hope night after night,
The year and the sun are aging.

Forest leaves rot in the mud,
Winter is on the road.
Outside the window, damp grass glistens;
October rain falls like arrows.

October 1936

Ji Xian

(Chi Hsien, b. 1913)

Lu Yu, who writes under the name Ji Xian, was born in Hebei but spent
his youth in Yangzhou, in Jiangsu Province. He graduated from the
Suzhou Institute of Art in 1933. After he moved to Taiwan in 1948, he
taught at Chenggong Boys' High School in Taipei until he retired for
health reasons in 1974. Since the end of 1976, Ji has been living in
California.

   Ji started writing poetry at the age of sixteen; while still on the
mainland, he published several volumes (under the pen name Luyishi),
as well as edited poetry journals with fellow poets like Dai Wangshu, Xu
Chi (b. 1914), and Du Heng (1907–64). In 1953 he founded the
Modern Poetry Quarterly, which folded in 1964 but was revived in
1982; and in 1956 he founded the Modernist school, which advocated
"horizontal transplantation"—that is, importing Western models of
poetry—over "vertical inheritance," or learning from the native tradition.
Although disbanded in 1962, the Modernist school has had a long-term
impact on the poetry scene in Taiwan through its emphasis on artistic
experimentation.

BLUE BLOUSE

(The fading sunset in the alley
Brings a misty melancholy;
The fading sunset makes me sad,
As does my wife's pale face.)

Come back, I've been waiting for you.
I long to see your blue blouse.
Perhaps you'll grieve over my aging.
I'll reply: "It's the river wind that did it."
I'll tell you a few stories about the river,
And you'll listen quietly.
Then we'll both shed tears;
Yet how sweet the tears will be.

Come back, I've been waiting for you.
I long to see your blue blouse.

1934

HOME IN THE EVENING

In the evening, home takes on the color of dark clouds;
The wind comes to visit the small yard.
After counting all the homeward crows in the sky,
The children's eyes grow lonely.

At the dinner table my wife chatters—
Things from a few years ago are already hazy.
In the blandness of the green vegetable soup,
I taste a little of life's sadness.

1936

CITY ON FIRE

Looking through the window of your soul
Into that deepest, darkest place,
I see a city with no one fighting the fires,
And rolling tides of naked lunatics.

In the endless surge I hear the resounding
Names of myself, my loved ones, my enemies,
The numerous living and dead.

But when I reply softly:
"Yes, I am here,"
I, too, turn into a horrible city on fire.

Ji Xian

A WINTER POEM

Hibiscus leaves
Yellow and drop one by one:
Rustling
Soughing
In the cold spell.
I, too, am deciduous
And never act like an evergreen.

YOUR NAME

Your name is like a pristine forest on fire

I carve your name
Carve it on a tree
On the evergreen tree of life
When it grows into a skyscraping tree
How wonderful
Your name will have grown, too

Grown big
Grown bright
Then I'll call your name gently
In the softest voice in the world
Call it gently every night

Write your name
Draw your name
Dream your glowing name:
Like the sun, like the stars
Like a lamp, like a diamond
Like fire sparks, like lightning—your name

A SCENERY WATCHER

I like to stand away from it
Far away, so I can
See the mountains
The sea
The scenery

Yes, I am a scenery watcher

I see humans, and human nature, too
I see the soul
And the body
I see the loneliness of saints and sages
All in all, I see cylinders, and flames
In cuneiform and diamond shapes
Slowly rising

As for me, I don't like to wear a hat of any shape
I don't wear a tuxedo and a top hat
Or a tweed, straw, or gauze hat
Or a cap, a fez, a beret
Or a scarf
Or a farmer's headgear
Or a crown of laurel
I just let my long hair free like palm leaves swaying
In the wind: rustling, whistling, sighing

BLOOD TYPE B

After a bath on a summer afternoon
I lay down to take a nap
Suddenly I realized how much this long skinny body
Resembled that of Jesus Christ
And I, too, could be betrayed
Could be crucified with nails
Then my type-B blood
Is also holy, pure, and noble
It must not flow in vain
How can it flow in vain?
Well, then, let it flow

PSYCHOANALYSIS OF PIPE SMOKING

Drifting up from my pipe
Is a mushroom-shaped cloud
A snake
A life buoy
And a woman's naked body
She dances and sings
Of the swelling of a dry river
And the destruction of a brigade of dreams

Wu Yingtao

(Wu Ying-t'ao, 1916–71)

Wu, a native of Taipei, wrote poetry in both Chinese and Japanese.

OVER A FIRE

Over a fire
Up a ladder of daggers
Doing a primitive sword dance
A banner of command in one hand
He chants the names of a myriad gods
Accompanied by somber cymbals and drums

In Shalun
A fishing village of no more than thirty households
With an ancient shrine of patriarchs
Old men and peasant women wear innocent expressions
Young men with bare feet carry statuettes on their backs

The sacrifice has begun
Gods have descended
Led by the priest, the group walks over a charcoal fire
Up the ladder of daggers more than fifteen feet high
On the protective spells on the daggers

Climbing up, then down
Their feet tremble a little
But are not hurt
High is the sky
Far is the sea

Somber the cymbals and drums
Folks from out of town look on
The villagers are no heretics
They believe in their gods
It's been like this for centuries
Each year their gods are manifested in them
In their ancestors
In them

THE RUINS

Something happened here
In a neglected corner a rock stands
There are no mourning banners
No morning sun

Something really did happen here
Walls with bullet holes
Earth eroded by blood
Wind and rain inscribed on the bleak ruins

Perhaps the sickly mutt knows something
Perhaps the gray clouds or the withered flowers do
There must have been some mistake
Or some act of inescapable fate

In a few years, a few decades, from now
People will run to the borders once more
This is an age that counts wars with numerals
Death spreads like a plague

And each time a tragedy ends
People return to their homes one by one
And set up a gray memorial
In another new ruin

Chen Jingrong

(Ch'en Ching-jung, 1917–89)

A native of Sichuan, Chen started writing poetry in 1935–36 while auditing classes at Qinghua and Beijing universities. In the 1940s she was associated with the group of poets later known as the Nine Leaves. She served as an editor of *World Literature* magazine from 1956 until she retired for health reasons in 1973.

NIGHT VISITOR

The fire lies dormant in the ashes.
Whose fingers knock off cold dreams?—
A tap on the narrow door

Listen to the watch ticking and pretend it's a train;
A long journey lies under my pillow,
A long solitude.

Please come in, midnight visitor.
Perhaps you are a cat or a bug
Knocking on my lonely door each night.

All is gone: the tap on the door, the wind on the roof.
I love the landscape of dreams—
Who is tapping in my dream again?

Winter 1935

TO XINGZI

I shall walk toward you in August;
We shall listen peacefully
To the September twilight rain.

Chrysanthemums will bloom,
Chrysanthemums will wither;
Go to the banks of time
And build a dam.

Go cry by the dam
Over youth and love,
Go to the distant sea to find . . .

Will you throw it away, or will you keep it?
In the invisible wind, in the lightlorn darkness,
Chrysanthemums will bloom,
Chrysanthemums will wither.

May 22, 1942

DIVISION

I often pause for
A passing wind;
I often get lost
In the sound of a bell.
A cloudless blue sky
Makes me wistful, too.
I drink the same greenness
From a blade of grass or a pine.

Boats are ready for launching,
Wings are waiting to spread.
A bewildered bow
Sends an arrow flying.
On the night of a fire alarm,
Shadows are on the run.

Before familiar things
We suddenly feel like strangers,
Divided sharply
From the universe.

UNKNOWN CITY

I often see myself
As another unknown existence
Pondering unknown thoughts.
While I stand on a street corner
The wind gusts.
I watch a strange me
Vis-à-vis a strange world.

Many familiar things—
The clothes I wear,

The house I live in,
Books I love to read,
Music I love to listen to—
Don't really belong to me.
Even my body, my limbs,
My voice,
My walk,
Are an accident among the commonplace.

Space and time
Are occupied by me
And lost haphazardly.
How can I boast
About giving everything I have,
Even though on the stage of life
I play the tragic roles of receiver and giver?

I do not belong to me.
When I write short verses
Or long letters,
I am merely trying to weave a shred
Of warm sunshine from my dream
Into someone else's thought.

November 26, 1947

Mu Dan

(Mu Tan, 1918–77)

Mu Dan is the pen name of Zha Liangzheng. Mu was born in Tianjin and started writing poetry while he was a student at the Nankai High School. He entered Qinghua University in 1935 and graduated from Southwest United University in 1940, then stayed on as a teaching assistant. He matriculated at the University of Chicago in August 1949 and, after receiving an M.A. in English, returned to China in 1953 to teach at Nankai University. Mu was persecuted during the Anti-Rightist Campaign and the Cultural Revolution but was rehabilitated the year after his death. In China, Mu Dan is better known for his translations of Pushkin, Byron, Shelley, Keats, Eliot, and Auden than for his poetry.

A DISCHARGE

The destroyer of cities returns,
A faceless soldier is a person again.
The war has given you too much loneliness, yet you recall
The joy the company of steel brought you.

Here, there is nothing: the strange remains strange,
There are no fiery words to die for
Nor fast intimacies or childlike audacity
To break up the mediocrity.

Nor is fantasy born of danger.
Accustomed to acceptance, people wait selfishly
And rot, without the means to make a living.
The protector of the city is back in his mother's bosom.

Death is your past; now you long for rebirth.
Before, you parted against your will,
But our victor returns to see failure.
Bestower of peace, you cannot

Get used to peace, so you break it apart;
You cannot return each day to the same thing.
You are completely unprepared, surviving companion of the dead;
Your enemy lurks in a future good life.

You are groping, but there is no comparison.
When your immense purpose suddenly came to an end,
You went back to being natural, back to a void.
Alter your uniform, blood-roiling dreamer;

Although it is worn-out, maybe you are better off wearing it.
It is easier. In the past you had the pleasure of sacrifice;
Now you just have everyday life. Now you must pick up
What you once left behind, even though you are one of us.

My brother, you have worked hard; you become a stranger
When you reminisce on those famous places you once went.
Because you returned from a blunder of a war—
Humankind, including yourself, erred—you receive an unforgettable
  honor.

April 1945

Mu Dan

EIGHT POEMS

1

Your eyes witness a fire;
Although you cannot see me, I lit it for you.
Your years of maturity, and mine,
Are burning. Mountains stand between us.

In the natural course of metamorphosis
I fell in love with a transient you.
Even if I weep, turn to ashes, and am born again,
Girl, it is only God playing a trick on himself.

2

Sedimented between mountain boulders,
We grew in the womb of death;
A changing soul with innumerable possibilities
Can never hope to complete itself.

I converse with you, trust in you, love you,
And at such moments I hear the Lord snickering.
He constantly adds more yous and mes
To enrich us, to make us dangerous.

3

The tiny beast of your years
Breathes like spring grass,
Bringing your color, scent, and fullness
And making you wild in the warm darkness.

I walk through your marble temple of Reason,
Cherishing the life buried in it.
A prairie rises when our hands touch;
Therein lies its obstinacy, my delight.

4

Silently we embrace
In a world illuminated by words.
Dreadful is the amorphous darkness
Where the possible and impossible bewitch us.

And suffocating us
Are sweet words that die before they are born.
Their apparitions hover, making us slip
Into the freedom and beauty of confused love.

5

The sun sets, a breeze blows over the fields,
An ancient reason stands here.
That which moves the scenery moves my heart,
Flowing toward you, sleeping peacefully, from the oldest beginning.

That which forms the trees and steadfast rocks
Will make my desire last forever.
All the beauty it reveals
Will teach me how to love you, how to change.

6

Sameness and sameness blend in boredom;
Between differences strangeness congeals.
On a narrow path fraught with danger
I create a self to travel.

He exists, he obeys my commands;
He protects me yet leaves me in solitude.
His travail is to seek endlessly
For order just to abandon it.

7

Storm, distant road, lonely night,
Loss, memory, enduring time—
All the fears that science cannot dispel
Lead me to find comfort in your embrace.

In your ungoverned heart
Fair images go away as soon as they appear.
There I see your solitary love
Standing tall, rising parallel to mine.

8

No closeness can be closer;
All coincidences are fixed between us.
The sunlight through lush leaves and branches
Shines alike on two hearts of the same shape.

When the season comes, we shall fall.
But the giant tree that gave us life is evergreen.
Its cruel mockery of us (and tears for us)
Will turn into peace in its aged roots.

I

Severed from the womb, deprived of warmth,
I am an incomplete part longing to be rescued.
Forever alone, locked in the wilderness,

I am apart from the whole in a still dream,
Pained by the river of time, nothing within reach.
Endless memories cannot bring back my self.

When meeting another part of me, we weep together;
In the ecstasy of first love, I try to break out of the cage,
Stretching out arms to embrace myself.

The fancied image is but deeper despair;
Forever alone, locked in the wilderness,
I resent Mother for driving me out of dreamland.

VALEDICTION

How many youths have been intoxicated here
Before they set forth on the crowded road?
In the mists of your indolence and the clouds on the water
The selves that they have lost will soon be forgotten.

How many times have you opened the gate to your garden?
Your beauty is rich, but your heart has become cold,
Although the songs of the seasons are pleasing
In a night heavy with wingless dew.

When you are old and alone by the fire,
Then you will remember a reticent soul
Who once loved your infinite changes;
When the traveler's dream shatters, he loves your endless sorrow.

SELF

Not knowing which world was his home
He chose this language, that religion.
Pitching a temporary tent on the sand
Under a tiny star,
He began to trade feelings with things in the world—
        Not knowing if that was indeed me.

On the journey he encountered an idol,
Then assumed the role of worshiper.
Calling these friends, those foes,
Displaying joy, anger, sorrow, and delight where they ought to be
In the magnificent little shop of his life—
     Not knowing if that was indeed me.

After a time of success he went bankrupt
Like a dynasty toppling.
Things were indifferent, taunting, and punitive,
But he lost no more than a crown.
When sleepless at midnight, he felt despondent—
     Not knowing if that was indeed me.

Another world posted a notice for a missing person.
His absence had caused the shock of an empty room
Where another dream awaited his dreaming
And rumors awaited his fabrication.
All suggested a biography not yet finished—
     Not knowing if that was indeed me.

1976

Zheng Min

(Cheng Min, b. 1920)

A native of Fujian, Zheng studied English literature and later philosophy at Southwest United University. After graduating in 1943, she studied at Brown University, then transferred to Illinois State University in 1950, receiving her M.A. in English the following year. In 1956 she returned to China, where she has been teaching at Beijing Normal University since 1960. She started writing poetry in 1942 and belongs to the Nine Leaves group.

One of her poems refers to *Selige Sehnsucht,* a German work by an unknown author, whose title means "desire for happiness." All the poems are selected from *Collected Poems of Zheng Ming, 1942–1947,* published in 1949.

Zheng Min

ENCOUNTER AT NIGHT

I would not raise my hand to knock
For fear the sound would be too harsh.
A returning barque
Raises no oar;
It only waits for the ocean breeze at night.
If you are sitting under the lamp
When you hear my breathing outside,
Put down your cigarette,
Push open the door without a sound.
You will see me waiting there.

AFTER READING *SELIGE SEHNSUCHT*

New sprouts from the same old tree,
Wisdom from the same heart and soul,
Feelings are captured through the same window—
If death and change are precious, it is because
They are tied to eternal changelessness.

The earth stays the same as the seasons rotate;
Humans are alike in the river of history.
When two lives are united by a profound, lasting meaning,
They are the earth, they are humanity.
In the vicissitudes of time and space,
They are God, ideas, and eternal changelessness,
Surrounded by wind and snow, age, sunshine, and darkness
That dance like falling leaves; yet they stand in the center,
Two evergreen bodhi trees, constantly
Radiating the light of life.

Carrying the wholeness of the past, life proceeds
Like an ever-flowing river,
In the same position, with the same relations,
Allowing the soul to grow like an old tree.
Always evolving from the same point, life
Is the continuation of strength;
The visible present contains
Every invisible past,
And from all the past comes the metamorphosis of transcendence.

We stand high on a mountain rock and gaze at the rolling tide—
Behind the moving white line
Lies all the might of the sea.

Is there a flame worth our pursuing yet
Not ignited within the human heart?
Is there a night of love wholly dark,
Meaningless, and to be renounced
Yet enabling us to rise above our lives?
People pursue wisdom and freedom so hard
That they demand to see all living things
From the highest mountain peak.
For those pitiable people only, light
Is external, life is
Arranged, advancing is incited.
Has he who praises the moth ever
Abstracted the past from the present?
Life and striving will be
Like the flowing tide at sunset, silently
Retreating to the loneliest depths of the sea.

TREE

I have never heard sounds
Like a tree's—
When it is sad and blue,
When it is cheerful or in love.
Even on the darkest winter night
You should pass it by
As though passing by a people denied freedom.
Can't you hear the sounds locked in its blood?
When spring comes,
Each robust arm
Holds a thousand wailing babes.

I have never felt serenity
The way I feel
The posture of a tree.
No matter what thought I wake from,
I see it

Standing tall
As the stars revolve between its arms,
As brooks murmur beneath its gaze,
As birds fly to and from its bosom.
It is forever praying, reflecting,
As if growing in a tranquil land.

Zhou Mengdie

(Chou Meng-tieh, b. 1920)

A native of Hunan, Zhou graduated from the Kaifeng Normal School.
After he moved to Taiwan, he ran a bookstand in downtown Taipei for
many years. Now retired, he is a member of the Blue Star Poetry Club.
His name means "dreaming of a butterfly," an allusion to Zhuangzi
(fourth century B.C.), a Daoist philosopher who, upon awakening from
a dream, could not tell if he was Zhuangzi, who had dreamed of being a
butterfly, or the butterfly dreaming of being Zhuangzi.

DAGGER

1

Jump down from heaven
Shake a rusty arm

Put on a pair of wings
Fly toward the intersection
Buy a dagger
   A zither with no strings
   A jug of spring wine where winter is buried
   A key to the gates of Hell

2

I'd like to shrink the world
Into an orange blossom or an olive
So I can close my eyes, meditate, and regurgitate
When I am cold and hungry.

WINTER SOLSTICE

Too long have I roamed;
My zither, my sword, and my chastity are covered with dust.

Twilight on the crow's back is getting colder and heavier.
Why do they not come out—the lone star and clear moon that light my
    return?

A last will written in blood comes drifting down from the maple top;
In the wasteland the Creator sets autumn's mustache aflame.

"Finality" is about to brand your brow. Return,
Guard it carefully: your shadow is yours.

Lin Hengtai

(Lin Heng-t'ai, b. 1924)

A native of Zhanghua, in central Taiwan, Lin majored in education at
the National Normal University. A member of the Modernist school
in the 1950s, he cofounded the Bamboo Hat Poetry Club with Zhao
Tianyi (b. 1935), Wu Yingtao, Bai Qiu, Li Kuixian (b. 1937), and others
and started publishing the *Bamboo Hat Poetry Journal* in 1964. Before
the retrocession of Taiwan to China, he wrote poetry in Japanese; he has
published poetry volumes in both Chinese and Japanese.

SPRING

a long neck
humming a minuet
thus announcing
that which is being squeezed out
from the soft pipe
is spring

AUTUMN

a rooster
meditates with one leg up

its crown wholly red

therefore
autumn is deep

SCENERY

1

by the side   of
the crops   are more
crops   by the side
are more   crops
by the side   more

sunshine sunshine sunning its long ears
sunshine sunshine sunning its long neck

2

outside   the
windbreakers   are more
windbreakers   outside
are more   windbreakers
outside   are more

Yet the sea   and the ranks of the waves
Yet the sea   and the ranks of the waves

Luo Fu

(Lo Fu, b. 1928)

A native of Hunan, Luo attended Hunan University before he joined the military and moved to Taiwan. After graduating from the Academy of Political Commissars, he served in the navy. In October 1954 he and his fellow poets Ya Xian and Zhang Mo (b. 1931) founded the Epoch Poetry Club and published the journal *Epoch,* which is still in publication. Since the 1950s, Luo Fu has published ten volumes of poetry, as well as essays and criticism.

The title of "Song of Everlasting Regret" comes from the classic poem

written by Bo Juyi (772–846) about the tragic romance of Emperor
Xuan and Lady Yang. A rebellion broke out in 755; the capital,
Chang'an, was seized, and the emperor fled to the southwest. Halfway,
the imperial army refused to move on unless Lady Yang, allegedly
responsible for the downfall of the empire, was executed. The emperor
yielded, and she was strangled at Mawei Slope.

WINTER

The longan in the yard bloomed, vexing me,
So I cut it down and threw the wood in the fireplace.
That was the major event of last winter and half the spring.

The old leaf-sweeper next door bad-mouthed me behind my back with
   words I could not understand;
Birds composed songs to call me names, pecking at my maturing roses.
The sun was right to complain, for without trees, the sunset would lose
   its half-hidden beauty;
Without fruit, it could not show off the fullness of its existence.
(All this I recorded in diary thirteen.)

Winter came early this year, the cold wind tugging my hair and biting
   my feet.
Late at night I remembered those travelers from the south and the road-
   side inns,
So I stuffed my diary into the fireplace.
Let the person getting warm by the fire hate himself.

OUTSIDE THE WINDOW

Looking out my twilight-decorated window after the rain,
I measure the depth of the distant hills.

After puffing air on the windowpane,
I draw a slender boat with my finger
And, at the end of a narrow path,
A man's back.

February 14, 1956

DEATH IN THE STONE CHAMBER

6

If you are worried about my waking up,
Open the windows on the dying city.
No need to poke those words around in my beard:
They are dead,
Your eyes are their burial ground.

Someone tries to suck early morning light from my forehead;
He pounds on me and tries to shatter me like an iceberg.
By the fire, I watch myself melt into a spoonful of cold water;
I smile
As I flow into your spine, your blood.

15

If a grain of wheat cries under the millstone
And is crushed,
Then I experience being chewed,
I utter a cry as chilling as an iceberg:
"Oh, food, you are murdered in the storehouse of abundance!"

Summer's anxiety crawls on winter's forehead
Slowly across the glance between two walls, the glance
That hangs all over the room like ivy. When a myriad colors approach
  in silence,
When I am gloomy all day because I cannot forget trivialities,
I am called something trite.

1961–63

SONGS OF SAIGON

After the Coup
The motorcycle belongs to that Texan;
The dust belongs to me.
The sticks belong to those wild kids;
The blood belongs to me.
The sun belongs to the Buddhist monks and nuns huddled in the street
  on a hunger strike;
The hunger belongs to me.
The waters of the Saigon River belong to the sky;

The emptiness beyond my grasp and my bite, neither painful nor tick-
  lish, neither propitious nor calamitous, neither Buddhist nor Zen—
That belongs to me.

Sand Bags on the Execution Ground
One by one the heads march down the sandbags
And lean their ears against the ground.
They seem to hear someone singing a dirge for himself
On the other side of the earth.

The notice affixed to the stake is blown away;
A good-looking face
Vanishes from the mirror.

April 3, 1968

SONG OF EVERLASTING REGRET

That rose, like all roses, only bloomed for one morning.
—H. Balzac

1
From
The sound of water
Emperor Xuan of the Tang dynasty
Extracts the sorrow in a lock of black hair

2
In the genealogy of the Yang clan
She is
An expanse of white flesh
Lying right there on the first page
A rose bush in the mirror
In full flower, caressed by
What is called heaven-born beauty
A
Bubble
Waiting to be scooped up
From the Huaqing Pool

Heavenly music is everywhere
In Li Palace
The aroma of wine wafts in body odors

Lips, after being sucked hard
Can only moan
And the limbs outstretched on the ivory bed
Are mountains
And rivers too
A river sound asleep in another river
Underground rapids
Surge toward
The countryside
Until a white ballad
Breaks out of the soil

3

He raises his burned hand high
And cries out:
I make love
Because
I want to make love
Because
I am the emperor
Because we are used to encounters
Of flesh with blood

4

He begins to read newspapers, eat breakfast, watch her comb her hair,
   handle official papers in bed

                             stamp a seal
                             stamp a seal
                             stamp a seal
                             stamp a seal

From then on
The emperor no longer holds court in the morning

5

He is the emperor
But war
Is a puddle of
Sticky fluid
That cannot be wiped off
Under the brocade coverlets
Slaughter is far away

Distant beacon fires snake upward, the sky is dumbfounded
By heart-stopping hairstyles
Leather drums with flame-red tongues
Lick the earth

6
Rivers and streams
Burn between the thighs
War
May not be abandoned
Campaigns are affairs of state
My lady, women's blood can flow in only one direction
Now the armies refuse to budge
All right, all right, you are the willow catkins
Before Mawei Slope
Let the wind in the square hold you aloft
A pile of expensive fertilizer
Is nourishing
Another rose bush
Or
Another incurable disease
In history

7
Regret probably begins in the middle of fire
He gazes out the window into the distance
His head
Sways with the flight of birds
His eyes change colors as the sun sets
The name that he cries out
Sinks into the echoes

All night long he paces around the room
In front of every window in Weiyang Palace
He stops
Cold pale fingers nip the candlewick
Amid muffled coughs
All the begonias in the Forbidden City
Wilt overnight in
The autumn wind

He ties his beard into knot after knot, unties and ties it again, then
  walks with his hands behind his back, the sound of his footfalls
  footfalls footfalls, a tuberose exploding behind the curtain, then he
  stretches out all ten fingers to grab a copy of the *Annotated Classic of
  Waters,* the water drip-dripping, he cannot understand at all why the
  river sobs instead of bellows when it flows through the palm of his hand
He throws on a gown and gets up
He sears his own skin
He is awakened by cold jade

> A thousand candles burn in a thousand rooms
> A bright moon shines on the sleepless
> A woman walks toward him along the wall
> Her face an illusion in the mist

8

Suddenly
He searches in a frenzy for that lock of black hair
And she hands over
A wisp of smoke
It is water and will rise to become a cloud
It is soil and will be trampled into parched moss
The face hiding among the leaves
Is more despairing than the sunset
A chrysanthemum at the corner of her mouth
A dark well in her eyes
A war raging in her body
A storm brewing
Within her palm
She no longer suffers from toothache
She will never again come down with
Tang dynasty measles
Her face dissolved in water is a relative white and an absolute black
She will no longer hold a saucer of salt and cry out with thirst
Her hands, which were used to being held
Now point
Tremblingly
To a cobbled road leading to Chang'an

9

Time: seventh day of the seventh month
Place: Palace of Longevity

A tall thin man in blue
A faceless woman
Flames still rising
In the white air
A pair of wings
Another pair
Fly into the moonlight outside the palace
Whispers
Receding farther and farther away
Glint bitterly

An echo or two reverberate through the storm

September 1972

BECAUSE OF THE WIND

Yesterday I took a walk
Along the river
To where the reeds bend down to drink,
And I asked the chimney
To write a letter for me in the sky.
The scribble was a little hard to read,
But my heart
Is as bright as the candle by your window.
Any ambiguities
Are inevitable
        Because of the wind.

Whether you understand this letter is not important;
What is important is that
Before all the daisies wither,
You must, without delay, get angry or laugh out loud.
Find my light jacket from the chest,
Comb your soft black hair in front of the mirror,
And then, with the love of your whole life,
Light a lamp.
I am a flame
That might go out anytime
        Because of the wind.

January 8, 1981

Luo Men

(Lo Men, b. 1928)

A native of Guangdong, Luo studied at the Air Force Pilots' Academy
and served in the Civil Aviation Bureau in Taiwan. He is a member of
the Blue Star Poetry Club, a full-time writer, and the husband of the
poet Rong Zi.

"Years of Poetry" is dedicated to his wife, whom he married on April
14, 1955. The title of her first volume of poetry, published in 1953, is
Blue Bird. The Chinese transliteration of hamburger, *hanbao*, means
"Han fortress," hence the reference to a fortress in "Lunchtime at
McDonald's."

THE DRIFTER

exhausted by the sea, a ship lies in the harbor
he leashes his shadow to the coffee table with a lamp
it is his pet, following him everywhere
otherwise Nana is so close that nothing is farther

drinking wine until it turns into the moonlight back home
staring at the empty bottle until it turns into a deserted island
bringing his pet along
he walks toward his footfalls
a distant star is also
   carrying the sky along
tomorrow when the first window blinds
   pull the sun into a ladder
he is not sure whether to go up   or down

1966

UMBRELLAS

leaning out his apartment window
he watches the umbrellas in the rain
   turning one by one into
   a lonely world
he thinks of hordes of people
                rushing every day from crowded
                  buses and subways

    wrapped up in themselves as they hole up at home
                    and close the doors

          suddenly
all the apartments in the building
        run into the rain
yelling all the while that they too
          are umbrellas

he stands there, stunned
and squeezes himself into an umbrella handle
      but only the sky is an umbrella
         with rain falling under it
           while outside it is dry

1983

YEARS OF POETRY

Had the blue bird not come,
    How could the woods and fields of a clear spring day
      Have flown into the bright month of April?

Had flaming June not become a firebird,
    Arriving on a trail of myriad colors and lights,
      How could winged summer have crimsoned the maples on the twin
      hills
And handed their glorious beauty to autumn?

In the silent wilderness at dusk, the swan
    Left the last white blossom
      To light up a cozy winter.
        I pick up a handful of snow,
          A handful of silver hair,
          A handful of looks.
They become a river flowing back to April,
A poem to send back to April.

1983

LUNCHTIME AT MCDONALD'S

1

a group of young people
   rush in
   with the wind
are pulled over
   by the brightest seats
   sitting together
   with the entire city

a tray of food and drink inside the window
a view of the street outside
knife and fork flying
back and forth more speedily
than the crisscrossing traffic
     a brisk, cool
     noon

2

two or three middle-aged men
sitting in fatigue
the knives and forks in their hands
open out into pairs of chopsticks
taking them back to that shop thirty years ago
six eyes looking over
six bluebottle flies
     in a daze
the tabletop suddenly darkening into
     a tapestry of memory
that bottle of wine
   that tipsy conversation
and next thing you know
it's no longer noon

when gust after gust of young people
   blow in and out
   the automatic doors
you can hear the sounds
   of drifting leaves in the chilly woods

3
an old man
sits in a corner
in an ill-fitting
   ready-made Western suit
finishing up a not-too-palatable
   hamburger
try as he may, he just can't figure out what it has
to do with a Han fortress
a glistening rice paddy is no
glass high rise
he sits there idly like
an old pine tree that is part of the decor
it's all right when he keeps quiet
as soon as he starts talking
he ends up in a conversation
with deafening cannons
thus engaged
the bright noon at hand
is already twilight in view

1985

Rong Zi

(Jung Tzu, b. 1928)

Born into a Christian family in Jiangsu Province, Rong Zi, christened
Wang Rongzhi, received her education in China and moved to Taiwan in
1949. She started writing poetry in the late 1940s and published her
first volume, *Blue Bird,* in 1953—the first book of poems by a woman
published in postwar Taiwan. The wife of the poet Luo Men, Rong is a
founding member of the Blue Star Poetry Club and acknowledges early
influences by Rabindranath Tagore and Bing Xin. The following poems
are all from her 1965 collection.

Rong Zi

I WALK THROUGH THE SEASON

I walk through the season
And hear its murmurs of delight,
But to spring I belong no more.

I will walk straight through without looking back,
Heedless of the myriad green leaves calling to me
Or the profuse blossoms of late spring.

I walk through—
Yet know not where I'll stop.
When at the season's birth a sweet dream is sculpted into a bud,
Locking within it a bronze-colored heart—
I can only walk straight through, unable to look back.

REVERIE ON A WINTER DAY

That is a steady light, not a low-flying firefly
Nor a cold star, smiling in the fireplace.

Perhaps all will fade away in the flames.
Lingering grief is shed in the pure firelight,
For I've never walked among the thorns of a highland forest
Nor crossed Death's wasteland.

It's true, all is gone; latent sorrow,
Shadows, and cold dreams are all melted in the fire;
Only the soft flickering of the rose-colored flames
Skims across your face now and then like a flower-laden branch.

All gone! In winter
Before the dozing fire, nothing can be recalled,
Not even my zither,
Which once sang like birds in spring woods.

All are napping; by the cheerful fireside at home
War is a thing of the distant past—
In the sleepy firelight I, too, wish I could forget
That once-clamorous word.

MY DRESSER MIRROR IS AN ARCH-BACKED CAT

My dresser mirror is an arch-backed cat
That keeps altering its pupils,
So my image changes like flowing water.

An arch-backed cat, a wordless cat,
A lonely cat—my dresser mirror.
The eyes round with surprise hold a mirrorful of dreams.
Is it time, radiance, or sorrow
Flickering within?

My dresser mirror is a cat of fate;
Like a stern face, it locks my beauty
Within its monotony, my demureness
Within its coarseness. And now it has become as lazy and
Indolent as summer.

It has given up its rhythmic gait and is stranded there.
My dresser mirror is a squatting cat.
My cat is a mysterious dream without light or shadow—
It has never given me a truthful reflection.

FLOWERS NO LONGER FLY IN OUR CITY

Flowers no longer fly in our city in March
Monstrous buildings squat everywhere—
Sphinxes in the desert, squinting at you in mockery
And a pack of urban tigers howl
From morning to night

From morning to night
The downpour of pitch-black smoke, the thunder of the city
Squabbles between cogwheels
Conflicts between machines
Time broken into pieces, life fading away by the moment

At night our city is like a poisonous spider
Extending its web
To snare pedestrians

The loneliness of the heart
The emptiness of the night

I often sit quietly in the dreamless field
To watch the city at the bottom of the night, like
An incomparably large diamond brooch
On display in the window of an import boutique
Waiting for someone to pay an exorbitant price.

Yu Guangzhong

(Yu Kuang-chung, b. 1928)

Although his parents came from Fujian Province, Yu was born in Nanjing
and lived in Jiangnan, the South, before he moved to Taiwan. He
received his B.A. in English from the National Taiwan University and his
M.F.A. from the University of Iowa. He has taught in Taiwan, Hong
Kong, and the United States and is now dean of the College of Humani-
ties at the National Zhongshan University in Gaoxiong, Taiwan. He is a
founding member of the Blue Star Poetry Club.

"The Alley on Xiamen Street" is about an alley off a street in Taipei.
The traditional Mid-Autumn Festival, alluded to in the poem, takes
place on the fifteenth day of the eighth lunar month; celebrants view the
full autumn moon and eat "moon cakes." The stanza about the world
turned upside down mentions, among other events, the death of the
shah of Iran ("Pahlavi"), the devastation caused by an earthquake in
Tangshan, Hebei, in July 1976, and the arrest of "four prisoners"—the
Gang of Four, arrested after Mao's death in 1976. "Cow sheds" were
the places of incarceration for the "five black categories"—landlords,
rich peasants, antirevolutionaries, bad elements, and rightists—during
the Cultural Revolution.

DOUBLE BED

Let the war proceed away from the double bed.
Lying on your long slender slope,
I listen to stray bullets like a horde of shrieking fireflies
Whizzing above your head and mine,
Through my beard and your hair.
Let coups and revolutions shout around us.
At least love is on our side,

At least we are safe till daybreak,
When all will cease to be dependable
On your firm slope.
Tonight, though mountains may crumble and the earth quake,
At worst I'd fall into your long low vale.
Let banners and bugles be hoisted.
At least a six-foot-long rhythm belongs to us,
At least you are mine till the sun rises,
Still smooth, soft, and smoldering—
A pure, refined insanity.
Let night and death on the border of darkness
Launch the thousandth attack on eternity
While we spiral downward, heaven underneath,
Swirling into the whirlpool of your limbs.

December 3, 1966

FOUR STANZAS ON HOMESICKNESS

Give me a scoop of the Yangzi River, oh, the Yangzi
  River like wine
  The taste of drunkenness
  Is the taste of homesickness
Give me a scoop of the Yangzi River, oh, the Yangzi

Give me a red begonia, oh, red begonia
  Begonia as red as blood
  The scalding pain of seething blood
  Is the scalding pain of homesickness
Give me a red begonia, oh, red begonia

Give me a white snowflake, oh, white snowflake
  Snowflake as white as a letter
  To wait for a letter from home
  Is to wait feeling homesick
Give me a white snowflake, oh, white snowflake

Give me a fragrant plum blossom, oh, plum blossom
  Plum blossom as fragrant as Mother
  Mother's fragrance
  Is the fragrance of my native soil
Give me a fragrant plum blossom, oh, plum blossom

Yu Guangzhong

IF A WAR IS RAGING AFAR

If a war is raging afar, should I cover my ears
Or sit up to listen in shame?
Should I cover my nose or inhale
The stench of charred flesh? Should I
Listen to you panting of love or to stray bullets
Preaching the truth? Mottoes, medals, provender—
Can they satisfy insatiable Death?
If a war is frying people, if far away
Tanks are tilling the spring soil
And babies are wailing by their mothers' corpses,
Wailing for a blind and mute tomorrow;
If a nun is burning herself alive,
Her celibate flesh crackling with despair,
Her curling limbs embracing nirvana,
In an ineffectual gesture; if
We are in bed, and they are on the battlefield
Sowing peace among barbed wire,
Should I panic, or should I rejoice
That I am making love, not wrestling,
That it is your naked body in my arms, not an enemy's?
If a war is raging afar and we are there,
And you, a benevolent angel with immaculate white wings,
Bend over the sickbed to look at me,
Lying armless, legless, sightless, sexless,
In a field hospital reeking of blood;
If a war is raging afar,
My love, if we are afar . . .

February 11, 1967

FOLK SONG

They say there is a folk song in the north
Only the Yellow River with its lung power can sing
From the Blue Sea to the Yellow Sea
    The wind hears it
    The sand hears it

If the Yellow River is frozen into ice
The maternal, nasal sound of the Yangzi River resounds
From plateau to plain
  The fish hear it
  The dragons hear it

If the Yangzi River is frozen into ice
There is still me and my howling Red Sea
From morning tide to evening tide
  Awake, I hear it
  Dreaming, I hear it

If someday my blood is frozen too
Your blood and his blood sing in chorus
From type A to type O
  Crying, you'll hear it
  Laughing, you'll hear it

December 18, 1971

THE KOWLOON-CANTON RAILWAY

You ask me what Hong Kong is like.
Holding your aerogram in my hand, I smile sadly.
Hong Kong is a clanking rhythm, my friend,
Drummed on steel tracks by a thousand wheels,
From border to border, from sunrise to sunset,
North and south, back and forth, an endless nostalgic song.
Unbreakable, inseverable, it is a futile umbilical cord
Stretching into the northern wilderness,
Toward that loving yet unfamiliar mother's body,
To a land once joined, now long since set asunder.
It is an ancient cradle rocking in the distance,
Rocking your memories, my friend, and mine.
And, like all nerve-endings,
This railway is sensitive.
At this moment, on the platform,
Holding your letter and leaning against a lamp post,

I can tell, even with my eyes closed, that
The one tinkling in is a passenger train,
The one clanging out is a freight train,
The one with the suffocating stench—
Quick, hold your breath!—is a hog train.
September 29, 1975

THE ALLEY ON XIAMEN STREET

It's that season again, when the mid-autumn moon is almost full.
Autumn has arrived at the mouth of the alley, but summer is still
   lingering
In the shade of the broad-leafed trees at the end of the alley.
This is the most secluded place in the world.
Let me stroll through
The tunnel of time, with echoes like distant tides,
Only to see a youthful me, with a full head of black hair,
Walking this way from the end of the alley,
His eyes gleaming with desire for the world outside.
We meet halfway in the alley and stare at each other,
Feeling both familiar and strange.
"What is the world like out there?" he asks;
His look is eager but a little ludicrous, too.
"You'll find out when the time comes." I smile.
"Some things fall short; some
Are much more horrible than you imagine."

Early autumn weather is like an olive pit,
Round in the middle, pointed at the ends.
In the crisp mornings and evenings, on the golden wind
You can smell the mid-autumn moonlight and moon cakes—
The moonlight radiating across endless miles,
The winds hollow from half a lifetime overseas.

It's time for the moon of reunion.
The skinny woman at the grocery store greets me
With a neighborly grin:
"When did you come back from abroad?"
I don't know if my apartment for the past six years,
On a peninsula at the motherland's back door,

With its windows facing the ocean breeze and the North Star,
Should be considered home or abroad.
"How long have you been back?" In the market
The proprietor—now grown plump—weighs the cabbage as she directs
  the question
At my wife, carrying a basket, and me, following behind.

Isn't all this what one calls home?
When the world outside has been turned upside down,
When Vietnam is lost, Pahlavi dead,
Tangshan destroyed, China grown lean,
When the fat tyrant lies in a crystal casket
And four prisoners squat in the new cowshed,
Only this quiet September alley is left,
Half awake, half asleep, in the ripe autumn sun.
Let me amble within,
Like an insect back in the grass, a fish at the bottom of the sea.
Even if I could go back to Jiangnan,
Where the red flags flap in the autumn wind,
How many old men have survived the disaster
And, sitting on the stone bridge over the canal,
Wait for me to return
For dinner in an unfamiliar home?

September 14, 1980

Yang Huan

(1930–54)

Yang Sen, whose pen name is Yang Huan, was born in Liaoning and
moved to Taiwan as an army corporal in 1948. On March 7, 1954, he
died in a railway accident in downtown Taipei.

Yang Huan

HOMESICKNESS

A long time ago, I was a king, happy and rich.
The princess next door was my beautiful wife.
We harvested pearls of sorghum, jewels of corn,
And all those gold coins hanging from the old elm tree.

These days? These days I don't have a penny.
Popular songs and neon lights make my mind anemic.
Standing at the schizophrenic street corner,
I don't know which way to go.

I AM BUSY

I am busy.
I am busy

Wielding the blowtorch,
Molding myself,
Beating the parade drum and cymbals,
Playing the spring-saluting reed pipe,
Releasing forecasts of happiness,
Collecting news of the truth,
Transplanting trees of life into the jungles of war,
Brewing yeasty blood into the wine of love.

Not until the day I die,
Like a fish sleeping in a smiling pond,
Will I turn out the light to rest,
Will I have a beautiful completion,
Like a volume of poems:
And the great earth that covers me
Will be the book's cover.

I am busy.
I am busy.

A DYING STAR

Gently
With a silver paper-cutter
I'd like to cut those veins like blue rivers
And let melancholy and grief
Rage forth.

Faced with a dying star,
I forget the tears inching down my face.

SLEEPLESS NIGHT

Tonight once again
I am excused from incarceration in painful sleep;
In the dark room
I light up.
With cigarettes, like so many pieces of chalk,
I write life's questions and answers
In silence
On the blackboard of night:
Beautiful tales and lines of poetry.

Guan Guan

(Kuan Kuan, b. 1930)

Guan Guan is the pen name of Guan Yunlong. A native of Shandong, Guan served in the Nationalist army, moved to Taiwan in 1949, and was discharged in 1978. He has held various jobs in the broadcasting and film industries. In his own words, his profession is "writing, acting, painting, and falling in love." He attended the International Writing Program at the University of Iowa in 1982.

The subject of one poem, Xue Tao (768–831), a famous poet, was a courtesan in the Tang dynasty (618–907). Widely admired by the poets of her day, she was also known for the fine paper she made, which she called "fir flower tablets." A poem dedicated to her by a contemporary refers to her residence in a loquat lane, and the phrase "loquat lane" has become a euphemism for a brothel. In the same poem, Xue is referred to by the official title of "proofreader," which subsequently became a euphemism for prostitute. Song (960–1279), Yuan (1280– 1367), Ming

(1368–1643), and Qing (1644–1910), like Tang, are names of major Chinese dynasties. Lines 9–10 of the poem are a quotation from the famous lyric poem "Lady Yu," written by Li Yu (937–78).

YOUNG TREES IN AN EMPTY FIELD

1

whenever I see
a few
skinny
little trees
standing
in the wind
in the setting sun
in an empty field at the far end of the sky
I wish I could run to where the trees are
and gaze at them

although
where they stand I would see
a few more
skinny
little trees
standing
in the wind
in the setting sun
in an empty field at the far end of the sky

although
I wish I could run up
although

in the empty field at the far end of the sky
there may be
a
tower

although the runner
seems smaller and smaller
as he runs

like a star

2
whenever I see
a few
skinny
little trees
standing
in the wind
in the setting sun
in an empty field at the far end of the sky
I wish I could run
and stand
with the trees

like a horse
or
stand
with the trees

and weep

1970

LOTUS FLOWERS

"There used to be lakes of mud here."
"You mean these plots of lotus flowers?"
"Now they are rooms of swamps."
"You mean these ponds of buildings?"
"Are they ponds of buildings?"
"No, they are houses of lotus flowers."

XUE TAO IN THE LOQUAT LANE

May I ask, Comrade, is the Xue Tao who wrote poetry home in the
  loquat lane?
May I ask, Comrade, is she who looked at hibiscuses from a riverside
  pavilion here?
May I ask, Comrade, is the woman who rinsed flowers in the Flower-
  Rinsing Stream here?

May I ask, Comrade, is Proofreader Xue, who made "fir flower tablets,"
  here?
May I ask, Comrade, is Xue Tao, who drew wellwater to make paper,
  here?

"Comrade, she is here, though she is no longer the Xue Tao from long
  ago.
I don't mean the long ago of Tang, Song, Yuan, Ming, or Qing;
I mean the long ago of long ago."

I see. "The carved railings and jade steps still remain,
  But the Fair One is not the same."
  "Long ago" is locked in Xue Tao's well,
  But none can see it.
  Xue Tao is standing on Xue Tao's paper,
  But none can touch her.

1991

Shang Qin

(Shang Ch'in, b. 1931)

Luo Yen first published under the name Luo Ma, then adopted the pen
name Shang Qin. A native of Sichuan, he joined the military at an early
age and moved to Taiwan in 1949. He attended the International Writing
Program at the University of Iowa and has been assistant editor in chief of
China Times Weekly. He is now retired.

    A Lian, the subject of one poem, is a small town in Gaoxiong Prefec-
ture in south Taiwan. Its name means "lotus."

GIRAFFE

After the young prison guard noticed that at every physical examination
  all the increases in the prisoners' heights were in their necks, he
  reported to the warden: "Sir, the windows are too high!" But the reply
  he received was: "No, they are looking up at Time."

The kindhearted young prison guard did not know the face of Time nor
  its origin and whereabouts, so night after night he patrolled the zoo
  and waited outside the giraffe pen.

Shang Qin

FUGITIVE SKY

The faces of the dead are a swamp seen by no one
The swamp is a piece of escaping sky
The fugitive sky is roses overflowing
Spilled roses are snow aborning
Snow aborning is tears in the veins
Flying tears are lute strings being plucked
Twanged strings are a burning heart
A charred heart is a swamp

FIRE EXTINGUISHER

At noon when anger arose, I glared at the fire extinguisher on the wall.
A child came up to me and said: "Look! There are two fire extin-
guishers in your eyes." Because of his innocent confession, I pinched
his cheeks and smiled, and could not help crying. I saw two mes crying
separately in his eyes. He did not tell me how many hims he saw in the
mirrors of my tears.

A FARAWAY LULLABY

Languidly
    perhaps   it is raining on the island
    salt   is drying on your pillow
    outside the salty window   night watches
    night   night will watch over you

    watch over soil   watch over salt
    watch over you   watch over trees
    for soil   watches over trees
    for trees   will watch over you

    for trees   will watch over the night
    birds in woods   watch over trees
    birds in trees   watch over stars
    stars in the night   watch over you

    for stars   will watch over night
    clouds in the sky   watch over stars
    clouds amid stars   watch over wind
    wind in the night   watches over you

for wind   will watch over night
grass on the ground   watches over wind
grass in the wind   watches over dew
dew in the night   watches over you

for dew   will watch over you
watch over soil   watch over trees
watch over mountains   watch over fog
fog in the night   watches over you

fog in the night   watches over rivers
water in rivers   watches over fish
watches over mountains   over shores
mountains by the sea   watch over you

mountains in the night   watch over you
mountains in the night watch over the sea
watch over beaches   watch over tides
ships in tides   watch over you

watch over tides   watch over night
watch over beaches   watch over you
watch over shores   watch over water
I in the night   watch over you

watch over mountains   watch over night
watch over soil   watch over you
watch over stars   watch over dew
I in the night   watch over you

watch over woods   watch over you
watch over grass   watch over night
watch over wind   watch over fog
I in the night   watch over you

watch over sound   watch over night
watch over birds   watch over you
watch over wars   watch over death
I in the night   watch over you

watch over images   watch over you
watch over speed   watch over night

watch over shadows   watch over darkness
I in the night   watch over you

watch over solitude   watch over night
watch over distance   watch over you
I in the night   watch over night
I in the night   watch over you

A LIAN

If it is night, A Lian
In the darkness warm as your womb
I can light up a thought
To brighten the only brook
Flowing through your soft fine hair
Swimming fish, with your tawny tail
You beat against the left chamber of my heart
Making me throw up nearly half a spring
(It was November
      of last year)
The fake spring of November
Sneaks around
I don't know why I want to laugh
If they cut the corner
Off your street, there will be two corners
Spring is oval
Winter has been cut again and again

If you use your tawny fins to hit me
You will be embraced, A Lian
Your ears will be nibbled
(Turn that red handle)

If there's no night, A Lian
If day doesn't come and dusk is gone forever
If in the endless dawn
Lilac breasts are adorned with dying fish
Someone's arms will petrify on the pillow
Someone's neck will be carved in relief there
Salt will crystallize and be smashed by a meteor

If it is night, A Lian
Villagers will raise naked bamboo poles and hang
Countless prayer lanterns capped with sugarcane leaves
They see how the darkness in the quiet courtyard
Is polished into a lusterless black gem
By those lights
I cross my green arms over it
And die there. But
A Lian, you don't know that someone's spying on you
Someone carves some new names with the wind
Inside your belly
In the darkness warm as your womb

A Lian, turn that red handle
Otherwise I shall hear you elsewhere
Where they dye tears in pretty colors
And hang them at the door by the stringful to separate cold from warm
On the metal tailgate of a gasoline truck
I hear how you are frightened
Cut in half by the tree shadows on the sidewalk
And trampled by hurtful words
No longer embraced, no longer nibbled on

January 27, 1958

ELECTRIC LOCK

Tonight the street lights where I live went out at midnight as usual.

While I looked for my key the kindhearted taxi driver aimed his head-
lights at my back as he backed up. The glare ruthlessly projected the
inky silhouette of a middle-aged man onto the steel gate. It was not
until after I had found the correct key on the bunch and inserted it
right into my heart that the good fellow drove off.

Then I turned the key in my heart with a click, pulled out the delicate
piece of metal, pushed the gate open, and strode in. Soon I became
accustomed to the darkness inside.

January 13, 1987

Ya Xian

(Ya Hsien, b. 1932)

Ya Xian is the pen name of Wang Qinglin. A native of Henan, Ya joined the military as a young man and moved to Taiwan in 1949. After graduating from the Drama Department at the Military Intelligence Academy, he served in the navy. He was a cofounder of the Epoch Poetry Club, attended the International Writing Program at the University of Iowa, and received his M.A. in Chinese from the University of Wisconsin-Madison. He is now editor in chief of the literary supplement of the *United Daily News,* the largest private newspaper in Taiwan, and teaches modern literature at Suzhou University.

The party mentioned in his poem "Salt" is the Nationalist Party, or Guomindang. It led the revolution of 1911, in which the Qing dynasty (1644–1911) was overthrown and the Republic of China was founded. Wuchang, in Hubei Province, is the city in which the final uprising took place.

"On the Streets of China" contains a number of classical and other allusions. Nuwa is the creator goddess in Chinese mythology. The Yellow Emperor is the legendary ancestor of the Chinese people, Luozu is his wife and the inventor of sericulture, and Ciyou is his archenemy, whom he defeats. Shennong is the mythic inventor of agriculture and herbal medicine, Fuxi the mythic inventor of the Chinese written language and the eight trigrams—the divinatory symbols used in the *Book of Changes,* or *Yijing.* Oracles, the oldest extant Chinese writing, were inscribed on tortoise shells and ox bones. The *ding* on which the wheat is cooked, is a bronze tripod used in imperial sacrifices during the Shang (1766–1122 B.C.) and Zhou (1122–256 B.C.) dynasties. Two important places are mentioned in the poem: Dunhuang, a city in west China on the Silk Road and a storehouse of Buddhist scrolls, paintings, and sculptures dating from as early as the fourth century, and Qufu, the birthplace of Confucius (551–479 B.C.), in present-day Shandong Province.

SALT

Second Auntie had never met Dostoevsky. In spring she called for only
one thing: "Salt, salt, give me a handful of salt!" Angels sang in the
elm tree. That year the sweet peas barely bloomed.

An official of the Ministry of Salt led a camel caravan by the edge of the
sea seven hundred miles away. No seaweed had ever reflected in Second

Auntie's sightless eyes. She cried for only one thing: "Salt, salt, give me a handful of salt!" Angels giggled as they shook snow down on her.

In 1911, Party members came to Wuchang. But from behind the foot-binding cloth hanging from the elm tree Second Auntie doddered into the panting wild dogs and the great-winged vultures. Many voices drifted away on the wind: "Salt, salt, give me a handful of salt!" That year almost all the sweet peas put forth white blossoms. Dostoevsky never did meet Second Auntie.

January 14, 1958

ON THE STREETS OF CHINA

Dreams are moonlight's blotting paper,
Poets wear corduroy,
Public phones are not connected with Nuwa,
Thoughts walk on a path of oracle bones,
After eating with the Muses a meal of wheat cooked in a *ding*
It is lonely to eat sandwiches and steaks,
And poets wear corduroy velvet.

The Yellow Emperor cries out:
"Trolleys have replaced our phoenix carriages.
Now that there are gas lamps and neon lights,
We cannot borrow our old sun.
Let us recall the fierce battle with Ciyou
And the beautiful silk song of Luozu.
Let us recall that poets did not wear corduroy!"

There were no problems before there were city councils;
Confucius did not worry about Laozi's copyright.
Airplanes screech over a row of willows,
Student protests surge against the crumbling palace walls.
Without coffee, Li Bo could still write poetry and didn't start a
  revolution—
Let alone not wearing corduroy.

Whitman's leaves didn't come from Dunhuang,
Ocean liners say there are four seas beyond the four seas,
Beggars in the subway extend their grimy bowls,
Sailors flirt with scantily clad women.

Turn left: red light, turn right: red light,
And poets wear corduroy.

An advertisement for a cure-all is pasted over Shennong's face;
At the first sign of spring, arguments about intergalactic travel break out;
Steam whistles strangle workers, pamphlets on democracy, bus stops,
   lawyers, electric chairs;
No more decapitated heads are on the city gate;
Fuxi's eight hexagrams were too early to win a Nobel Prize;
The red cedars in Qufu are used for railroad ties.
What to wear? Corduroy.

Dreams are moonlight's blotting paper,
And poets wear corduroy.
They say dragons never existed,
So let us eat with the Muses a meal of wheat cooked in a *ding*.
Let us think about walking on a path of oracle bones,
Let us wait for an erotic film to end,
And let us wear corduroy.

November 1958

ABYSS

I want to live, there is nothing else. At the same time I've discovered his
displeasure.
—Jean-Paul Sartre

Children often get lost in your hair,
The first spring torrent, hidden behind your barren pupils.
Fragments of time shout; the body spreads out, becoming a nighttime
   carnival.
In the venomous moonlight, in the delta of blood,
All souls stand erect and pounce on the face
Drooping on the cross.

This is absurd. In Spain
People wouldn't even throw him a cheap wedding cake!
We wore mourning for all, spent the whole morning touching a hem of
   his shirt.
Later his name was written on the wind, on a banner.
Later he cast us
His life, the leftover meal.

Go look, pretend you are blue, go smell putrid Time;
We are too lazy to know who we are,
Working, strolling, saluting the wicked, smiling, and being immortal—
The ones who cling to mottoes.
This is the face of day. All the wounds whimper, teeming viruses hide
  beneath the skirts.
A metropolis, scales, a paper moon, mutterings of power lines,
Today's notice pasted over yesterday's notice,
The anemic sun trembles now and then
In the pale abyss
Sandwiched between two nights.

Time, time with a cat's face,
Time, strapped to the wrist, semaphoring,
On a rat-wailing night, those long since killed are killed again.
They tie a knot with cemetery grass, grind the Our Father to a pulp
  between their teeth.
No head will rise among the stars
Or cleanse the crown of thorns with gleaming blood.
In the thirteenth month of the fifth season, heaven lies below.

And we build monuments to the moths of yesteryear. We are alive.
We cook wheat with barbed wire. We are alive,
Passing through the sad tunes, the squalid shadows on the cement,
And the souls released from prisons of ribs.
Hallelujah! we are alive. We walk, cough, debate,
Shamelessly occupy a corner of the earth.
Not much is dying at the moment,
Today's clouds plagiarize from yesterday's.

In March, I hear cherries calling out.
Many tongues shake loose the debauched spring. Blue flies nibble at her
  face;
Her legs swish between the high slits in her dress; she hopes someone
  will read her,
Will go inside her body to work. Except for this and death
Nothing is certain. Living is a wind, living is the sounds on the threshing
  grounds,
Living is pouring out the desire of an entire summer
To them—those women who love being tickled.

At night, beds sag everywhere: the sound of light in a fever
Walking on broken glass, a confused tilling by coerced farm implements,
A translation of peach-colored flesh, a horrible language
Pieced together with kisses, a first meeting of blood with blood, a flame,
   a fatigue,
A shove, pushing her away.
At night, beds sag everywhere in Naples.

At the end of my shadow a woman sits. She is weeping;
A baby is buried between Indian strawberry and Aaron's-beard.
The next day we go see the clouds, laugh, drink plum juice,
And dance away the remnants of our integrity on the ballroom floor.
Hallelujah! I am still alive. The shoulders carry the head,
Carry existence and nonexistence,
Carry a face wearing a pair of trousers.

Whose turn is it next time? I wonder. Perhaps a church rat's, perhaps
   the sky's.
We have long since said farewell to the much-hated umbilical cord.
Kisses imprinted on the lips, religion on our faces,
We carry our coffins as we wander about.
And you are the wind, the birds, the sky, a river without end,
Ashes standing erect, death not yet buried.

Nobody can pluck us up from the earth. We see life with our eyes closed.
Jesus, have you heard the jungles humming in his brain?
Somebody is drumming under the sugar-beet field, somebody is
   drumming under the myrtles.
When some faces change color like chameleons and their eyeballs
Stick to the darkest pages of history,
How can rapids retain reflections?

And you are nothing.
You do not break your cane on the face of the age,
You do not dance with dawn wrapped around your head.
In this shoulderless city, your book is torn up on the third day to make
   paper.
You wash your face with night sky, you duel with your shadow,
You live on an inheritance, on your dowry, on the faint cries of the dead,
You walk out of the house and then walk back in, rubbing your hands.
You are nothing.

How can you make the legs of a flea stronger,
Inject music into a mute's throat, or let blind people drink up the light?
You sprinkle seeds on your palm, squeeze moonlight from a woman's
  breasts,
Enter the layers of night revolving around you.
Bewitchingly beautiful, they are yours—
A flower, a jug of wine, a bed of seduction, a day.

This is an abyss between the pillows and the sheets, as pale as an
  obituary couplet.
This is a sweet-faced woman, this is a window, a mirror, a tiny powder
  compact.
This is laughter, this is blood, this is a satin bow waiting to be untied.
That night, Maria on the wall ran away and left behind an empty
  picture frame;
She went looking for the Styx to wash away the shameful things she had
  heard.
And this is an old story, like a twirling lantern: senses, senses, senses!
In the morning when I hawk a full basket of sins,
The sun pierces my eyes with spikes of wheat.
Hallelujah! I am still alive,
I work, stroll, salute the wicked, smile, and am immortal,
I live for living's sake, watch clouds for the sake of watching clouds,
Shamelessly I occupy a corner of the earth. . . .
By the Congo River lies a sleigh;
Nobody knows how it slid that far.
A sleigh that nobody knows.

May 1959

COLONEL

That was another kind of rose,
Born of flames.
In the buckwheat field they fought the biggest battle of the campaign,
And his leg bade farewell in 1943.

He has heard history and laughter.

What is immortality?
Cough syrup, a razor blade, last month's rent, etc., etc.
His wife's sewing machine skirmishes,
While he feels that only the sun
Can capture him.

August 26, 1960

AN ORDINARY SONG

By the star thistles is an elementary school, farther down is a mill,
Next door is Auntie Su's garden, where mustard greens and corn grow;
To the left of the three maples are a few other things,
Farther down, the post office and a tennis court, with a bus stop all the
 way to the west.
Clouds float above the clothes drying on the line;
Sadness may be hiding by the railway.
It's always like this.
May is here.
Accept these things quietly, do not make a fuss.

At a quarter to six, a freight train passes by.
The river under the bridge ties a pretty knot and flows away. When grass
 takes off to occupy the distant graveyard,
The dead never look around.
And the most important thing is,
On the balcony there
A boy is eating a peach.
May is here.
No matter whose rafter eternity nests on,
Accept these things quietly, do not make a fuss.

April 1965

Zheng Chouyu

(Cheng Ch'ou-yu, b. 1933)

Zheng Chouyu is the pen name of Zheng Wentao. A native of Hebei,
Zheng was born into a military family and accompanied his father on
campaigns all over China. After moving to Taiwan, he graduated from
the National Zhongxing University and worked at Jilong Harbor in

north Taiwan for many years. In 1968 he attended the International Writing Program at the University of Iowa, from which he received an M.F.A. He has been teaching Chinese at Yale University for many years.

The "General's Order" mentioned in one of his poems, "A Fortress in Ruins," is the title of a classical poem originally set to a tune. His "Bloody Eclipse" was written after the June Fourth Massacre at Tian'anmen Square in 1989. Grove Street Cemetery, the subject of another poem, abuts the Yale University campus. It has been the burial place of local celebrities since colonial times. The former president of Yale University A. Bartlett Giamatti is buried there; he died in 1989.

A FORTRESS IN RUINS

The guards have gone home, leaving behind
A border fortress in ruins.
A prairie of the nineteenth century is
Nothing now but a stretch of sand dunes.

The tip of an arrow,
The nail where once a bugle hung,
Cobblestones on the tower
Smoothed by nightfalls and homeward-gazing boots—
All is old,
All rusty with wind and sand.

Where a century ago heroes tied their horses,
Where a century ago warriors honed their swords,
I unload my saddle with a heavy heart.
There is no key to history's lock,
No sword in my pack.
Let me ask for a clangorous dream—
In the moonlight, I issue that mournful "General's Order"
From the strings of my lute.

THINKING OF A FRIEND AT YEAR'S END

This year the mercury drops to the bottom line.
How I miss that year—
My wool jacket at the pawnshop,
Doors and windows sealed tight by a snowstorm.

Thenceforth even good friends were like
Mercury, dropping
To zero.

If I had been born ten years earlier,
If I had breakfasted at noon,
If my wife had returned to her family more often,
If I could have worn that gray wool jacket
While walking in the snow,

Then I would have a purer, more carefree
End of the year;
Then it would be time
For pines to look for bamboos,
For bamboos to look for plum blossoms,
For me to be alone at your graveside,
Tromping out a zero with my feet.

The wool jacket was a gift from you;
In return I bade you farewell with a whole night of drinking.
That year the old snow was still deep
When new snow fell.
I watch as the circles of footsteps around
The grave fade away . . .
The slow
      drop to
          zero.

NIGHT-BLOOMING CEREUS

I am a blind man
As I listen to my wife and my daughter describe the
Delicate blooming of the cereus.
I search in what I hear
For the recorded sound of the petals opening

And discern the sound of a star falling,
A rainbow vanishing.
("The flower withered abruptly.")
I hear, too,
The rise and fall of the moon.

Then I get up,
Rolling my sightless eyeballs slowly
In search of the satyr who sneaked into the flower and ate it.
How could my wife, my daughter, and the cereus
Know
These things?

1982

BLOODY ECLIPSE—RETURN TO THE EON OF THE FIRST CREATION

Quietly, the icy clear moon
Held the erupting volcanos in her arms,
Waiting for the flames and lava at her breast to cool down
With crackling sounds like jade breaking.
God said: Such is a mother's love for the created earth.

The green land became the Americas,
The blue land, Europe,
The golden land, Africa of the meandering coastline,
And Asia was the land of
Black and red.
The moon receded to where she could not be eclipsed.
God said: Love and peace be on earth.

Only one volcano refused to cool down,
        A crazed volcano under a curse,
Neither active nor inactive,
Both red and black—
That was China,
The only innocent land,
Forever primitive, forever savage,
Forever defying the mother, the moon.
It splashed blood on heaven and earth just to show her, to apply rouge
  to her cheeks.
God said: How bright is the bloody eclipse of the moon in China.

1989

Zheng Chouyu

GROVE STREET CEMETERY

1

The child sits on a broken tombstone
And tells stories
To an audience of the dead,
Who lean their ears out of the earth
Like flowers in bloom.

In the noon sun the shifting tree shadows
Make brush strokes
On the child's chest—
A fresh funerary inscription
  Written in the ancient seal script.
  (Another member of the human race leaves his name behind.)
In the noon sun the dark tree shadows sweep
And erase
    the funerary inscription.

2

The setting sun mixes
New autumn pigments on the stone wall.
Within, the plants and flowers have not yet been covered with frost.
Their array of colors
Recalls a chorus of children in their favorite outfits.

Grove Street Cemetery
Is like a small neighborhood
Where residents look out for each other—
  The tombstones cast their shadows
  On one another.
In the poet's corner
Mr. Giamatti's new tombstone
Has yet to be erected.

Through the centuries
Generations of birds have chirped;
Humans are much slower.
Students with backpacks full of books
Trundle along on their bikes. Are they contemplating
Their future or how to climb the
Stiff slope ahead?

At the top of the slope stands the gate of the cemetery.
On its plate is inscribed this tenet from the Scriptures:
The Dead Shall Be Raised—
Every time the scholars look up
Inside or outside the wall,
They smile a knowing smile.

1991

Bai Qiu

(Pai Ch'iu, b. 1937)

He Jinrong, who writes under the name Bai Qiu, was born in Taizhong
and graduated from the Taizhong Business Academy. He makes a living
as an interior designer. A founding member of the Bamboo Hat Poetry
Club, he has been a member of the Modernist school and the Blue Star
Poetry Club as well.

In "The Wanderer," *silk fir* is the Chinese name for the sawara false
cypress.

LAST NIGHT

the one who came and left last night
the one who talked about the forlorn autumn wind
last night
the one
who smiled at me
with moonlight
on rippling water
the one who
walked across my heart
with the footsteps
of falling leaves
the one who
gave me pleasure last night with a cat's warmth
last night's clouds
alas, the one who came and left last night

Bai Qiu

THE WANDERER

a silk fir gazing at the distant clouds
a silk fir gazing at the clouds
a silk fir
silk fir

       a

       s
       i
       l
       k

       f
       i

on the horizon r on the horizon

his puny shadow, his puny shadow
he has forgotten his name, forgotten his name, just
standing there   just standing, alone, lonely
standing   standing
standing
facing the east

     a solitary silk fir

A THOUSAND PATHS, A THOUSAND ROOTS—
IN MEMORY OF MY DECEASED PARENTS

A thousand paths—each is calling me
A thousand roots—each is calling me

But the path by which I came
Is buried in the wind and the dust
The roots from which I sprang
Are rotted
Only I am left
In this hurly-burly world

Only I

THIS IS BEYOND MY CONTROL

I attend the same bed as you;
Sometimes, though, I secretly lock you out of my dreams.
This is beyond even God's control:
Kissing, making love, and, afterward, fatigue.

(I'm so sorry. She is not you. My apologies.)

This wound came before your time;
It smarted every now and then.
Living on little Xinmei Street,
I have devoted a long life to you.

This is beyond even my control:
Spitting, coughing,
Blowing my nose,

Thinking—in a remote town
She is lying in a stranger's arms.

WITHOUT END

How long can they hold on
Sensing that root tips have begun to rot
Incapable of carrying the weight of life
Like the gloomy darkness of the womb
Without end

Rest awhile
At the bottom of the world's deep night,
Listen to the sperms
Crying for help as they bob in the river

As death's sorrows
Rise in the chest

WILD GEESE

We are still alive, we still want to fly
In the boundless sky.
The horizon cowers in the distance, luring us on
To live, to pursue.
We feel we are getting closer, but when we look up, it is still far away.

The sky is the one our ancestors crossed,
Vast and empty, like an unchanging exhortation.
Our wings are the ones our ancestors had, surging against the wind;
We carry on, determined, trapped in a nightmare.

Between the black earth
And the azure sky,
The future is a streak of horizon
Beckoning to us.
We shall gradually die in pursuit, die like
The sunset growing cold. Still, we must fly,
Staying aloft in the boundless sky, solitary as a leaf in the wind.

And the cold clouds
Watch us askance.

THE SQUARE

the crowd of men broke up in a hubbub
      and went back to bed
   to uphold women who smell good

while the bronze statue holds staunchly to his ism
facing an empty square
his arm raised, shouting

the naughty wind
kicks at the leaves
to wipe away the footprints

Fang Qi
(Fang Ch'i, b. 1937)

Fang Qi is the pen name of Huang Zheyan. Fang, who was born in
Taipei, graduated from the National Taiwan University in 1962. He
received his Ph.D. in physics from the University of Maryland in 1973
and now teaches there. A legend among poetry circles in postwar
Taiwan, Fang was a hermit during the 1960s, according to Ya Xian.

  The Frenchman mentioned in "Composition" is Jules Supervielle
(1884–1960). He was born in Uruguay but received his education and

lived much of his life in France. Primarily known as a poet, he also wrote novels, short stories, and plays.

All the poems except "Snowman" are from Fang's 1966 collection, *Dirges*.

LITTLE BOATS

> lonely little boats are moored aslant
it's the same on all the beaches in the world
> and like heads at a slant
> they brim with sadness

ON THE SEA

dusk at sea, where cloud cattle and cloud sheep cannot dwell
> their watery hoofs cannot rest on
> the inhabitable green sea-prairie
> dusk at sea is no dwelling place

GUARDIAN ANGEL

for each city, each bridge, each person, there is a
> guardian angel, hanging three feet overhead
under the dim light, we sit down at a round table
> have a seat, guardian angels, and chat awhile

WINTER CURFEW

Dost thou know the power is cut off and the night curfew has begun?
> Dost thou know that I can shut my eyes and make the rain stop?
Dost thou know God on the wall puffs out air to keep Himself warm?
> Dost thou know the flag of love is hoisted over every bed?
Dost thou know the pillow is a ferryboat rowing toward dreams?
> Dost thou know my dreams are an old quilt covering thee?

COMPOSITION

at the bottom of the closet a lock of hair a book of poetry a yellowed
poetry manuscript a program a ticket stub and a dimly shining silver
coin chaotic like my brain empty like your universe

          the music hall resembled
the abdomen of a giant beast baskets of flowers and the words on a
lantern a black piano on the stage the white dress to the right he
tossed a coin to decide whether to walk over much later she happened
to leaf through *Gravity* and found among its pages the short poem
"Fire" only then did she recognize the strange look in his eyes that
night it was Supervielle who once lent his Frenchman's eyes like
binoculars so they could look out the same window and watch the
city on the flatlands at the far side of the sky all this is enough for a
story and if one adds the lock of hair she gave him on the eve of their
parting it is even more complete

          is this all there is

why not

at seventeen the age of tea and sympathy on the morning of her
birthday she cut a lock of black hair as a memento and for her
birthday he searched the city found a volume of *Gravity* in that tony
used-book store yet was too timid to send it he was able only to write
a poem secretly in class he found out indirectly that she played the
piano took a risk and mailed her a concert ticket when strains of
music wafted from the depths of the cave he looked at the vacant seat
next to him and suddenly decided to pursue the matter after the con-
cert he picked up a phone nearby yet could not bring himself to
deposit the silver coin he still remembers that red phone booth under
the yellow streetlights looking like a shrine that could accommodate
an outpouring of prayer and grace

SNOWMAN

1

        only someone who has an ice-cold hand
          can catch hold of winter's tail
          can refuse the eaves' protection
            and not tremble
          at the howling of dogs

only someone whose internal undertow is frozen
can understand loneliness
can stare at the dazzle on white snow
and not weep
at the jumble of footprints

powdered snow roils like a tiger
chasing, pouncing to kill
displaying the shape of the wind
who knows that a snowman
wants to learn to speak too
needs love too
is secretly in love with the sun

2

memory is an exquisite snowman, saying
I am made of the same stuff as the earth that bore me
a snowman is like a spermaceti candle
shedding tears of wax as it dies

sun god candlelight snowman
half of him searches for the morning sun in the haze
the other half turns into dark water
all that is left
we cherish in our hearts like an ice prairie

Published in 1972

Ye Weilian

(Yeh Wei-lien or Wai-lim Yip, b. 1937)

Born in Guangdong and raised in Hong Kong, Ye received his B.A. in
English from the National Taiwan University, his M.F.A. in creative
writing from the University of Iowa, and his Ph.D. in comparative litera-
ture from Princeton. He is a professor of Chinese and comparative liter-
ature at the University of California, San Diego, a prolific translator of
traditional and modern Chinese poetry, and a literary critic, in addition
to being a poet.

"Waterclock at night" is the name of the tune for a poem that was
meant to be sung.

THE STORY OF WILDFLOWERS

Wildflowers
Bloomed passionately
After the cannon fire had ceased.
Spring rain swelled
Streams of blood and hatred.
The roots of hope
Cried in the ruins,
Echoing faintly.
Pain,
Like the plowed soil,
Grew stout in the season's wind.
On the slopes—
"Wildflowers as red as fire!"
The song,
Like wave after wave of wheat,
Rose to the hilltop.
Many years later,
Old men in the village
Relay it in their various artful ways
As they sit on the stone bench under the banyan tree:
"The cannon fire was really caused by a radical climate change,
And hatred was required by the plot of the play."
Their slow, gentle southern lilt
Transforms the hurried cannon shots
Into a soft jingle.
The audience
Sheds a sympathetic tear
For the dead soldiers on both sides,
For they say
Death is real and unalterable.
"The cannon fire was really caused by a radical climate change,
And hatred was required by the plot of the play."
The audience
Sways in excitement
As the southern voices rise and fall.
Only I, who don't know how to treat reality as fiction,
Run straight to the hilltop, gather an armful of wildflowers,
Which is like holding a blood-stained soldier,

And stand still on the crest—
"Wildflowers as red as fire!"—
As the singing
Surges
Like wave after wave of wheat.

September 1974

SONG OF THE WATERCLOCK AT NIGHT

The high-voltage motor is hushed
Outside the wall
Delicate white flowers fall
Without a sound
From the tree
Late at night
The manufacturing district
Is empty
Like
A wind
Blowing through a huge brass pipe
The moon
Leaps up
Startling
A flock of sleeping gray pigeons
In the attic of the men's dormitory
Coo coo
Coo coo
Like the
Intermittent
Dripdrops
From a water tower

SONG OF THE LAKE COUNTRY—
THINKING OF FRIENDS IN THE SOUTH

This is indeed a rare
Flower in half bloom—
A slender petal of water

Next to a wide petal of rice paddies,
Interlocked with the petal
Of a soft brook
Holding a petal
Of fragrant rice stalks
While a petal of jumping fish
Embraces a petal of hopping sparrows.
In the spring
If you follow me
Deeper into the flower,
You'd better hold your breath
And pay close attention—
At the tip of the pistils
Within the petals of water
Within the petals of rice stalks
Within the petals of water
Is a rocking skiff.
On the skiff
Is a southern girl,
Rosy and fair,
Fair and sweet,
Sweet and soft,
Soft as water.
You and I had better hold our breath
On this unusual spring day.
Together we will keep the capricious wind and rain at bay
So that she can use her gentle power
To melt away the savagery of history
And the occasional rudeness and recklessness
Of you and me.

Lin Ling

(b. 1938)

Lin Ling is the pen name of Hu Yunshang, or Helen H. Ong. Lin was born in Sichuan and spent her childhood in Xi'an and Nanjing. She received her B.S. in chemistry from the National Taiwan University and her Ph.D., also in chemistry, from the University of Virginia. She now lives in the United States. Lin is a member of the Modernist school.

Mount Qilian and the Geng River, mentioned in "Non-Modernist Lyricism," are in northwest China. Chinese manuscript paper has six hundred squares, twenty-four across and twenty-five down; one ideograph is written in each square, much as English words are written on lined paper.

UNMOORED BOAT

There is nothing to make me stay—
Except for my destination.
Despite roses, green shade, and serene coves on the shore,
I am an unmoored boat.

Perhaps some day,
When I am tired of wandering in outer space,
On a blazing twilight in May
I will awake,
And so will the sea.
The world and I will renew our link,
And I shall return to the bounded world from the boundless, then
Quietly leave again.

Ah, perhaps someday . . .
I am willpower, I am an unmoored boat—
Although I do not have wisdom,
Neither do I have ropes or masts.

1955

RICE PADDY PATHS

You are vertical, I am horizontal;
Between us we determine the four cardinal directions.

We came from where we came, we passed,
And we met. After all, we did meet,
Surrounded by the contour ridges in the wet rice paddies.

An egret alighted.
We chatted, then said good-bye.
In silence we made a pact as we gazed at the distant twin peaks.

(A pure white feather came floating down.)

When a feather floated down, how we wished
Happiness were a white bird—
A feather dropped—so we made a wish,
Even if it came with wings.

1956

MINOR ENLIGHTENMENT—WRITTEN FOR A GAMBLER

In your bosom, O Monte Carlo night,
      the one I love is toasting himself by the fire.

The pine branches he has gathered are not enough, Monte Carlo night;
      so he takes my hair,
          my spine . . .

1956

SNOW-COVERED GROUND

1

On the snow-covered ground I lie supine
On the snow-covered ground
That glistening silver is love's bleached bones

You stroll along
I am sound asleep. I thought
Hyacinths in the Southern Hemisphere
Were still roaming

2

Ah!
A burial of long ago
Some frozen passion and severity—some
Bleached bones of love

At night
You pass by here on your way home
You love to whistle softly
And sit down by the roadside
How warm it is here, you think

It has a silver sheen
You seem to have been here before

What are you thinking?
I am sleeping here
Here on the snow-covered ground are love's bleached bones
I will collect your footsteps

3
Do you like to tramp about? Oh, yes,
I recall the slushy tracks you left behind on the heights
I have the pleasure of being ravaged
If you come here with your rusty skates
What am I—
I am mud, I am drops of melting water

NON-MODERNIST LYRICISM

That region is uninhabitable,
But I call it home.
It gave me the first longitude and latitude of
My existence to the north of the Tropic of Cancer.
On that primeval land
I set my feet time after time,
But I left it in the end.

I remember sacrificial animals were not prayed to there,
Brocade scrolls were not inscribed in the wilderness under the starry sky,
Blood
Was not shed in pledge—
Pledges were sworn with bones.
But the deboned Modernists
Will not, and cannot,
Be lyrical.
I mean lyrical in the most self-willed sense,
        (I mean lyrical in the most self-willed sense,)
Like an infant taking its first steps, alone
In a late spring field,
With an uninhibited urgency—
I mean like an infant isolated
        By sleep

And time
From all demeaning reasons,
Concepts, and canons,
Its genealogy traced to
The mountains and fields. Let the wind from Mount Qilian
Stop awhile, then ferry across the Geng River.
Let the wind from Qilian instruct, with all that is fit
      for harmony
       or all the unfitting
Restraint and indulgence.

     (I mean . . . I mean a pledged
     Modernist will not,
     And cannot,
     Be lyrical.)

Even silence is unacceptable—
     Silence is intensity of the highest degree,
     Intensity is silence of the highest kind.
Even emptiness is
Unacceptable. Emptiness
Congeals
Into forms—easy to touch
     but hard to contain.
It erodes
My relaxed elasticity,
Plasticity, and hardness
     on the manuscript paper with
     twenty-four by twenty-five squares—
There, the past was my soil; I plowed and planted
Old seeds
Out of season.
Now it is a bed, it is rest, it is the forbidden room
In my nightmares.

There, every night I put old passions on trial,
Pondering whether I should set them free or execute them—
The final, unnegotiable

Executions . . . if I can find
An execution ground by the edge of a river
Next spring, on the first sunny day
After the first rain,

To put them to a slow death.

1981

Fang Xin

(Fang Hsin, b. 1939)

Fang Xin, who was born in Sichuan, graduated from Tamkang University in Taiwan with a major in English and received his Ph.D. in English from the University of Montreal. He returned to Taiwan in 1970 and taught at Furen University. In 1972 he emigrated to the United States, and now he lives in California.

MOONRISE

Sunset sky—an immense silly grin
Above the roof on which a frisky redheaded boy is running
The moon he kicks up
   Is an empty pineapple can
   Clanking loud and clear

Published in 1963

A TELEPHONE BOOTH WITH AN OPEN DOOR

     A lonely young boy says:
Her laughter is a bunch of glittering silver coins
Dropping all over the floor with jingles and jangles.
But I am not a telephone booth with an open door,
Not in any way.
I can't even receive
One tiny coin of hope.

Published in 1963

RESURRECTION

All is quiet

The hammering on the stakes has stopped
Baby's crying has stopped
Automobile horns have stopped

I raise my hands and look up
At the sky of broken ice
There is not even a cloud
Not even a bird, not even . . .

A sprout of white bone
Breaks

Out of the purplish infected soil

Published in 1963

Xiong Hong

(Hsiung Hong, b. 1940)

Xiong Hong is the pen name of Hu Meizi, a native of Taidong. Xiong graduated from the National Normal University and has since been teaching at high schools. She attended the International Writing Program at the University of Iowa in 1974 and to date has published three volumes of poetry.

Beinan Creek, the subject of one poem, is, like her birthplace, in east Taiwan. The word *beinan* comes from the dialect of the aboriginal Ami tribe. The Zhan Che mentioned in the third stanza is a Taiwanese poet (b. 1954).

BOUND

I am the denizen of a cocoon—
You bind me with a thousand silken threads.
I cannot get out to observe life,
To observe my pitiful, petty life.

Standing on the bank,
How much heat can you feel
When I set myself on fire?
When I trudge barefoot in a snowstorm,

You stay outside the painting,
Viewing the snowy landscape.

A thousand threads, tears, loves—
I walk into the tightly woven cocoon,
Not wishing to observe life at all.

ENVOI

Love is a poem written in blood.
The blood of joy and the blood of self-abuse are equally sincere;
The scars from a knife and a kiss are the same—
So are sorrow and joy,
Compassion and hate,
For in love you must forgive both.

I am bowed down.
Fate has built a dry well with cold hard bricks
That wall me in.
Fate makes me cry a limpid spring
And will never release me,
Even if my flood of tears turns into a river
Because of my longing for you.

It must be so—
For Fate is absolute master,
For in love
The scars from a knife and a kiss are the same.
You must forgive both.

DEATH

picking up my hat quietly
I am ready to leave
there are many words—
only these will I say:
   in my next life I will still
   want to
   marry
   you

August 1975

Xiong Hong

TEARS

Because of tears like
Clumps of watercress,
I had to take the long way

Into the depths of that hill
Shrouded in mist—
Love and hurt
Spring from the same source.

August 1975

BEINAN CREEK

Beinan Creek is a long dark song
For people gathering wood in the driving wind and rain.
The water carries driftwood; one careless step
Of the bare probing foot will prove that
Life is no more than living.

I don't know how much a catty of firewood brings
Or how long a tree of an arm's girth can burn.
Look, the flood has come, folks cry as they
Wade panic-stricken through the water.
On a distant sandbar, the windbreak of horsetail wood
Has long since washed away. The flood has brought
Some driftwood, now stranded on the sandbar.
If the bare foot looking for a foothold
Is not careful, it will prove that
Life is no more than living.

Beinan Creek is a bitter song.
Zhan Che knows this; so do the children in Taidong to the west
(Lianxiang, you live in Hualian, so you don't know this),
Liushijianzai, Kitty Hill, and, farther back,
The aboriginal village behind the Girls' High School.
Intoxicating dances and songs
Under the harvest moon
In those happy days,
When the sun set in the mountains, the evening clouds
Appeared over the sea,
And wide rivers echoed

The spacious skies.
From the eighth through the twelfth grade, after school
I would sit and watch Beinan Creek,
Quiet, skinny Beinan Creek.
In those happy days
Beinan Creek was a carefree song.
On peaceful, ordinary days the creek
Was a thin river,
But after a rainstorm, it was like
A raging, galloping fire.
 (Memories that flared up like fire are ashes now.
 Whatever the song, sooner or later it will cool down.)

REMEMBRANCE

1
if you
if you have said to me
one or many
words of truth
when I wake up in the morning
I would remember them

youthful years
simple things
if you have said
one or many
easy or deep
cloud-flying, snow-falling words . . .

2
caring is asking
but sometimes
caring
is
not asking

if there is no news at all
like a calm sea after a ship
has sunk, that, too,
is a quiet remembrance

3
if at summer's end
or in early autumn
I have once or twice written
some oblique words
suggesting a certain incident
like an unexpected shower
that, too, is remembrance

Yang Mu

(b. 1940)

Wang Ching-hsien was born in Hualian, on the east coast of Taiwan. He received his B.A. in English from Donghai University in central Taiwan, his M.F.A. in creative writing from the University of Iowa, and his Ph.D. in comparative literature from the University of California, Berkeley. Currently he is professor of Chinese and comparative literature at the University of Washington. Wang, who now uses the pen name Yang Mu, published his first volume of poetry in 1960 under the pen name Ye Shan. He has published twelve volumes of poetry, in addition to essays and literary criticism in both Chinese and English.

The lama in "Lama Reincarnated" is Lama Tenzin Osel Rimpoche, who was two years old when the poem was written. When he was twenty months old, the Spanish boy was identified by the Dalai Lama as the reincarnation of an eminent Tibetan monk.

ON THE CLIFF

Then we came to the cliff where sunflowers bloomed everywhere, and
   We lay down, startling an early-returning partridge.
I pointed to the distant mountains and said, "Look at the lovely clouds.
   Springwater is dripping. Listen, listen to the woodcutter."

All day long we listened to the sound of wood being cut.
   The season had just begun, the forests were dense and deep.
Who would walk through that magnificent palace,
Through the thousand ancient Roman columns and spears,
   Watch wild wolves take human form,
    And sail the sea to reach the golden shore?
     One becomes a little homesick when the tide comes in.

You smiled and said, "But we're lying idly
On a cliff where sunflowers bloom everywhere.
We are only thinking about how to grow old quietly
And listening to the distant sound of wood being cut
While springwater drips through layers of rock."
We were up high, in each other's arms,
Lighting a fire, hunting, bathing, and growing old.

1963

TO TIME

Tell me, What is oblivion?
What is total oblivion? It is when dead wood
Is covered with the decrepit moss of a dying universe,
When fruits ripen and fall onto the dark earth
And summer turns into fall before they rot in the murky shadows,
When the abundance and crimson of the two seasons
Suddenly turn to ashes and dust
Under a slight pressure to break free,
When the blossom's fragrance sinks into the grass like a falling star,
When stalactites, drooping, meet upreaching stalagmites,
Or when a stranger's footsteps pass
Through the round, red-lacquered doors in a drizzle
And come to a stop at the water fountain,
Solidifying into a hundred statues of nothingness —
That is oblivion, whose tread leaves a ravine
Between your eyebrows and mine,
Like an echoless mountain grove
Embracing a primeval anxiety.
Tell me, What is memory
If you once lost yourself in the sweetness of death,
What is memory if you blow out a lamp
And bury yourself in eternal darkness?

1964

LET THE WIND RECITE

1

If I could write you
A poem of summer, when reeds
Spread vigorously, when sunshine
Swirls around your waist and
Surges toward your feet
Standing asunder, when a new drum
Cracks in the heat; if I,

Rocking gently in a skiff
Immersed to the twelfth notch,
Could write you a poem of autumn,
When sorrow crouches on the riverbed
Like a golden dragon, letting torrents and rapids
Rush and splash and swirl upward
From wounded eyes; if I could write you

A poem of winter
To finally bear witness to the ice and snow,
The shrunken lake,
The midnight caller
Who interrupts a hurried dream,
In which you are taken to a distant province,
Given a lantern, and told to
Sit quietly and wait,
No tears allowed;

2

If they would not allow you
To mourn for spring
Or allow you to knit,
If they said,
Sit down quietly
And wait—
A thousand years later,
After spring
Summer would still be
Your name—
They would bring you
Back, take away
Your ring

And your clothes,
Cut your hair short,
And abandon you
By the edge of the persevering lake—
Then you would belong to me at last.

You would belong to me at last.
I would bathe you
And give you a little wine,
A few mint candies,
And some new clothes.
Your hair would
Grow again, back to the way it was
Before. Summer would still be
Your name.

3

Then I would write you
A poem of spring, when everything
Begins anew.
So young and shy,
You would glimpse a reflection of the mature you. I would let you shed
   tears freely;
I would design new clothes and make a candle for your wedding night.

Then you would let me write
A poem of spring on your bosom
In the rhythm of a heartbeat, the melody of blood,
With the image of the breasts and the metaphor of a birthmark;
I would lay you on the warm surface of the lake
And let the wind recite.

December 1973

AUTUMN'S TEST

I hear the snapping of garden shears outside my window—
The sharp sound knocks about with pleasure in the wind.
The morning sun is sprinkled high and low, all over the grass and trees. I
Lift my head, distracted from my cup, and look outside,
Searching. The shadows on the wall are the color of tea leaves.
The shears cavalierly fly through low hedges and small trees.

A gentle, benevolent slaughter is going on
And on. I lean out the window; the sound
Suddenly grows louder, filling the neighborhood.
Yet there's no trace of the gardener.
The beech is laden with crimson nuts:
The leaves on the old maple seem ready to fall;
Behind the mossy path is the arbor of ripe grapes;
Beneath the pine tree lie two bundles of twigs;
Most of the chrysanthemums are in bud.
I walk into the garden, searching; there's no trace of the gardener
Inside or outside the walls. Only the morning breeze, sparkling, brushes
  by as if cooling a cup of tea.
The clacking shears are wielded by him. It's
The god of the seasons, testing me with the same sharpness and patience.

October 1985

LAMA REINCARNATED

A Tibetan lama passed away in San Francisco; some years later they realized
that he had been reincarnated in Spain.

They looked for me everywhere, starting out from Kashmir,
Going southeast along the Ganges
Through wilderness and villages, under the scorching sun, in rainstorms,
Past river gorges and mountain bends.

Then they split into two groups:
One crossed the Irrawaddy River, pushing anxiously
Eastward, across the Salween and the Mekong,
Searching at temples and pagodas everywhere.

The other group crossed the Indian subcontinent,
Turned to war-ravaged Afghanistan,
Enduring hunger, fatigue, and mistakes
Before they entered ancient Galilee.

When they entered Galilee with their alms bowls,
About to visit Jesus' birthplace,
Suddenly there was an explosion by the stone bridge—
A retaliatory bomb set off by terrorists.

They were completely mystified; gore
And violence are nowhere to be found
In our scriptures. They had no idea that
The eastward group had just arrived in Korea.

Pigeons fluttered in the tear-gassy air. Surrounded by
Riot police, a young student
Poured gasoline on himself and struck a match.
With a loud cry, he leaped back, trailing thick smoke and angry flames
  in his wake.

Then monks came out en masse, speechifying in the square
By turn, while the group left Galilee
Along the trail of the magi;
But in the hoary night they could not find the star.

They sat deferentially on the bus, hardly talking to each other.
Traveling day and night, they reached the seaside, boarded a ship,
And arrived at shore by following another myth. Ah, Europe,
With fig trees everywhere they looked, where could they find me?

At night they meditated by themselves. Outside the tavern
The nihilist Balkan Peninsula was in an uproar;
Wine flowed like fresh blood. They held a meeting
And decided to go north first to try the frigid zones.

They did not know that the other group
Had already changed planes in Tokyo
And crossed the Pacific and North America to enter
A Mexico that seemed to hold some possibilities.

They changed into their light yellow cloaks,
Hired a donkey cart, and visited many small towns.
Everywhere people played the guitar
As they sang over and over again: "Andalusia . . . "

The sea breeze fluttered against their searching eyes. In this way
They traversed many long and narrow countries.
Once in a while a few helicopters appeared in the sky,
Chop, chop, chopping Andalusia into pieces.

It was fortunate the other group
Decided to turn around when they got to the Baltic Sea.
Though they couldn't help getting lost in the Black Forest,
When spring came, they straggled into Morocco on foot at last.

They sat on the ground, depressed, not knowing where their next stop
Should be. To the east lay Italy (amen!),
To the west lay Spain (amen!). Church bells were
Ringing everywhere: Where could they find me?

Africa? Perhaps their reincarnated guru
Would appear in the Congo: a young lama of the Black Sect of Tantric
  Buddhism.
They got up, dusted themselves off, and decided on the spot
To board a ship and sail straight to Gibraltar.

That day they walked more than a hundred kilometers,
Thinking about the Congo all the while. They heard
Donkey hoofs clattering beyond the horizon.
Lovingly, the melodies of a guitar kept them company.

Someone was singing at ease under a fig tree:
"Andalusia . . . " The song
Arced across the parched plains. "Come with me,
Come with me to Andalusia."

They left the forked road. Lilies
Bloomed on the golden hillocks,
Sparrows flitted past, muskrats scampered
Among dry fields. I called softly to the wind:

"I am in Granada.
Bring me those insignia from a previous life:
My crown of gold, staff, rosary, and robes and cloaks.
Bring them to Granada, Andalusia."

By now the other group had traveled around
The tip of Chile. They, too, heard my whisper:
"I am in Granada." They looked left and right at the ocean:
"Granada? Ah—Andalusia."

Come, come, come to Andalusia.
Come find me, find me in faraway Granada.
Let us sing and praise eternal Granada,
A golden flower blooming in Andalusia.

Come, come, come to Andalusia.
Come find me, find me in faraway Granada.
Let us sing and praise eternal Granada,
Let us sing a new song about old Andalusia.

1987

Yang Mu

THREE ETUDES: THE SNAKE

1

Someone asked about something and,
Before I could answer, hid in the murmuring woods.
I looked around,
The greenness in my heart dissipated by the dappled light—
Heaven and earth were like a zebra.

So I stood quietly, thinking:
"His doubt was inevitable, even if
Tabooed." Then from a high treetop
A leaf came falling gently in E-flat,
Shaped like lips slightly open, swaying elegantly,
Fluttering, with delicate trills, through the brightest halo in a dazzling
  pose,
Alighting aslant on a spider web. Another
Mottled ray swept across one corner of the lips, illuminating them
In an instant. He asked about the train of my thoughts. Yet
He is rooted in a frigid, northern island in this stately forest,
A melancholy dissident in the
Cool shady depths of this forest,
Inclined to solitary living.

His palette—
Flying yellow and swift green, like the satin ribbons floating behind a
  Tang terra-cotta figurine.
He is a sash loosened from a woman's body after armor-clad midnight
When she awakes at the beginning of that shadowy year following the
  dragon.
Eyes gleaming with the cold light of a firefly, he examines his slender
  form
And is deeply shocked: "Beauty comes from time immemorial;
It is a mystical experience, fear inspiring,
With a touch of evil—but that is a misunderstanding."
Actually, except for shyness he has no flaws;
He is not even unsociable,

Though inclined to solitary living. That day
He swam to me swiftly in the grass, swooshing like a waterfall,
Assumed a soaring-swooping pose, and congealed
Into a sculpture of historical interest.
He seemed to be asking about my cares. While I hesitated

A leaf fell allegretto sforzando.
He turned around and retreated into
The depths of the forest—this melancholy
Dissident.

2

She may have a heart (the reeds shake their heads and look
Equivocal). If she did, it would be cold anyway.
I ran in the direction in which she vanished, and conjectured thus.
Under the cliff, the vines, the spring,
The noonday sun shone on the piles of pebbles now and then.
She sat cross-legged, furious and dejected,
Blaming herself in silence in a place no one knew.
Her ice-cold body doubled over, then doubled again.
Still she could not stir up a passion long dead; rather,
She realized that at a certain juncture below her head, where reason and
    emotion
Clashed, a spasm seemed to be occurring.
The timely spring drizzle drifting by was as warm as undried tears from
    a previous life.

She must have a heart, must have had one
Once, tightly wrapped inside her brilliantly colorful gown, beating,
Awaiting transmigrations and inevitable doom in some foreseeable age,
Dissolving somewhere to the left of the gallbladder.
And so she sat cross-legged on the pebbles, dejected and blaming
    herself. Why?
The reeds shake their heads equivocally.

3

So I conjectured, sitting in boredom
On a north-inclining cliff on this planet, listening to the tides pounding
    on the jumbled rocks.
I imagined snakes to be androgynous
Like angels. Lifting my head, I saw the clouds tumbling above:
Some were like gaily laughing faces, others like tightly knit brows.
I thought the androgynous snake
Must be an offshoot of a winged creature,
Especially since some are viviparous and some are oviparous.

Before the cool of autumn, the snakes completed their mating
In some bedewed wilderness.
The male slithered away from the spot, never to return—

Like grass decomposing into the ground, turning into mud, and then
    into fireflies —
Leaving the female alone, bewildered and uneasy, unsure
Whether to lay eggs this time or produce live young.
Falling into a deep reverie, she deliberated
And remembered:
How many painless moltings have I experienced?
In the hollow of an old tree, in a pile of dead leaves, in a barn or a
    deserted kiln,
Surrounded by chirping birds,
I have tried on my new gown in the soft spring breeze.
"Beauty is continuous creation, based on archetypes
Of something not deviating from the principle behind ancestral patterns
    and colors, et cetera." Yet beauty turns out to
Know no gender in her world, the world of
A species, once winged, that has
Evolved into crawling reptiles.

Even so,
The pensive snake could not help feeling resentful.
When the setting sun retreated from the surface of the water, leaving
Concentric ripples undulating in the fast-darkening bay,
And separated cosmic secrets with the seven primary colors
In an artful and dazzling moment.
Like angels, not bound by tradition or discipline or norms,
Invisible, indomitable, sounding clarions or caroling,
Having earned our respect and given us joy with their androgynous
    bodies,
She realized that his disappearance
Rendered her transformations meaningless. All this
I came to understand before I fell asleep.
Heaven and earth were like a molt.

August 1988

THE DAY AFTER EASTER

The day after Easter
I miss him and his atheism badly.
Pigeons fly across the sky outside the window;
Downstairs, shouts, each louder than the one before:

It is the minister's only daughter getting a crowd ready
To march together to the square.
The demure lily on my desk—
Like the swans, the pumpkins, and the king's deer
In legends—
Is heartbreaking. Last night
When I walked to the mouth of the alley with it, the Bible study group
Was still singing. The lights and music were equally steadfast and brave,
Proclaiming how long ago, in an obscure moment,
The Son of man came to life again and ascended into heaven.
This is the day after Easter,
Yet how desperately
I miss
His atheism
And him.

April 1990

IN LIEU OF A LETTER

Then the sky and the earth began to expand
Touching some reefs, islets
In the rolling and tumbling of gentle waves
In opaque, profound
Adulation: the heart is the universe's reflection.
We look for hidden teachings, send the scouts
On a detour, let love and hate follow against the current.
The distant hills slope gently;
A seagull unhurriedly
Flaps its wings, then swoops down;
So does another seagull with the same determination.

This is entirely possible, possessable—
Now as water vapor rises
And clings to our bodies.
Sunlight shimmers before us to the left,
Knocking against two pairs of dazed eyes
Like the moment our palms touch, the moment
Tears lie on the cheeks, wind blows across
The railing, blood surges into the heart,
Rain moistens the loquat blooming outside the balcony.

In silence I repeatedly arrange
One or two sentences. But
To finally give up without a word is most beautiful,
Though, wistfully, I had hoped to speak.
Then I think, If we just go on sitting here like this
On an idle afternoon,
Facing the intermingling sea and sky,
Cries of waterfowl
Coming from the pier now and then . . .
You blink your eyes, lean forward to search,
But the birds are gone
Already.

And so you are most beautiful, leaning against
A warm chair,
So peaceful, trusting, engrossed,
With no trace of calculation. Only when your will
In an undiminished fable
Gallops side by side with passion across hills and rivers
Through wind and rain, sunshine, moonlight,
Through feasts and adversities, are you most beautiful—in
A large illustrated book
The banner and armor of a vanguard,
Or in an encounter behind drawn curtains
When two gaze at each other prolongedly
Without sentimentality.

March 1991

Zhang Cuo

(Chang Ts'o, b. 1943)

Born and raised in Hong Kong, Zhang received his B.A. in English from
the National Zhengzhi University in Taiwan, his M.A. in English from
the University of Iowa, and his Ph.D. in comparative literature from the
University of Washington. He is now a professor of Chinese and com-
parative literature at the University of Southern California. Zhang,
named Zhang Zhen'ao at birth, started writing poetry under the pen
name Ao Ao while he was in college and later adopted the pen name
Zhang Cuo. His English name is Dominic Cheung.

The word for sonnet in Chinese, *shi si hang,* is composed of three characters meaning "fourteen lines," hence the question in the seventh sonnet in "Sonnets of Error" about how many words *sonnet* is.

SONNETS OF ERROR

1

The trouble is, once I write the first line
I know there are thirteen left;
Between the first and the fourteenth
Are those topsy-turvy lines in the middle
All at sixes and sevens.

In a well-designed landscape painting—
From the main peaks to the swirling cascades—
When will white clouds come drifting by,
When will the leaves fall in autumn?
Our love song

Has now come to the last quatrain:
Should I use an oblique rhyme,
Or should I follow the regular scheme?
Anyway, it is a sonnet of error.

2

Our falling in love
Is a sonnet,
Quite Shakespearean,
With rhymes in the first quatrain:
Together, apart, together, apart.

I know
The rhymes in the second quatrain are fixed, too:
To have, to have not, to have, to have not.

Are you really saying, Let's forget it?
And I, should I just forget it, too?

We cannot just forget it.
So long as heaven and earth endure
And sun and moon shine on,
We'll use the assonant *love* to rhyme our concluding couplet.

3

In the beginning there was no
Hint of a sonnet, let alone
Any intention of rhyming.
At that time it was
No more than a short and simple haiku.

But a mere seventeen syllables
Seemed such a protracted sonority,
Even though the notes were still,
And the rhythm of the heart was
Still five–seven–five.

In the end our resistance
Was no more than the space between stanzas,
A question you once asked me: When does it rain
On the quacking duck in spring?

4

All erroneous history begins with veritable facts;
They turn into historical errors
Only when they happen at the wrong time and place.

For example, Romeo and Juliet were happy
But in the wrong place and time.
They made the further mistake of falling in love:
Two errors put together,

Adding up to their correct deaths
When they handed their lives to the past,
Leaving the future to grieve forever.

That wretched embrace,
The despairing gaze—
Tears and blood fell line after line
Until they ran through all fourteen lines.

5

Although still wrong even after a lifetime of love,
We will never regret it
And will make the same mistake in the next life.

Anyway, it was preordained in our previous one—
The last embrace,
Also the first,

In the dark
Touching the paper autumn,
Paper maple leaves,
And myriad paper butterflies.

So don't ask me about the last kiss,
Because the lips are cold,
The tongue stiff,
The weeping stilled.

6

On the stone steps where we sat together
After you wept,
Moss appeared
In the span of one night
And spread to the spot
Where my iron fist struck.
Sorrowfully it spread along the crack,
Tracing it in green
Like an ice-cold green snake,
Wordlessly turning a certain night
Into a foreign land,
Into a zigzagging clue
For us in our next life when we
Wonder at a field of overgrown moss.

7

Is *sonnet* one word or three?
One line or fourteen lines?
Are there fourteen lines of one word each
Or fourteen words to every line?

When did the error begin?
Was it before the sonnet?
Or is *error* a noun,
Sonnet a verb?

Is the erroneous sonnet one sentence,
Or is it fourteen?
Or are there fourteen random sentences
On an erroneous topic?

The fact is: beginning with the very first stroke,
The error ran right through the last and fourteenth line.

April 9, 1979

ANCIENT SWORD

Long ago, I recall, you forged me.
You hammered away,
You burned my coal-black body
Until it flamed red.
The soaring ambition inside me
Turned bright and clear
With a tremor of the soul
As you poured a scoop of springwater over me.
You ground me, bent me, caressed me;
And at last, on a spring night in March,
With a flick of your fingers
I became a long sword, hard yet pliant.

I knew I was not your first forging;
Once forged, I prayed I would be your last.
With your gentle, skillful hands
Began the history of a steel sword,
A romance of countless temperings.
But now,
Hidden in the dark scabbard,
How shall I manage?
I have only one history,
But your love has a thousand faces.

Still, on every rainy night,
A certain loneliness sprouts in my heart,
Makes me restless,
And drives me to twitching and chanting:
The deep love of the ancient sword
Cannot be cultivated by a chivalrous spirit,

Nor can it be forgotten in the hurly-burly world.
There is a yearning
That spells cannot restrain
Nor rest subdue.
A question
Is repeated in the wind:
"Why did you make and then leave me?
Why did you forge my timeless love in steel
With your ephemeral flesh and blood?
Why did you, in the impulse of a short lifetime,
Leave me to eternal helplessness?"

1985

BEAUTY AND SORROW

I have come to realize
That the only beauty in life
Is to discover irresistible possibility
In the recognition of the possible and the impossible.
I could drive to a town ten miles away
On an overcast morning,
Sit sipping coffee or lemon tea
And listening attentively, in the faintly minty air,
To an internal monologue in one chapter of
The saga of a life approaching maturity—
Perhaps the voice speaks of a yearning for hearth and home
Or the pursuit of singleness.
Then, after a glass of white wine,
While spooning up French onion soup
Between the pink salmon and the white scallops,
I seem to see a crystalline teardrop
Brimming with love
Gently shed.
Poised at first between falling and not falling,
Between yes and no,
It, silently, for the beauty of a glance
Brimming with love,
Is gently shed.

Furthermore, I have come to realize
That the only sorrow in life
Is to discover sheer impossibility
Among limited possibilities —
As when, on an afternoon of pouring rain,
Any manner of embrace proves futile in the end,
Any vow of eternal love is but empty words.
Only in a certain shiver, bitter as lemon,
Is one reminded of the spring night in a hill town —
The taste of wine lingering on the lips,
The toothmarks of a midnight awakening still visible.
The perfume where she leaned against my right collar
Has been dissipated, slowly, steadily,
By the evening breeze after the rain
As though, in the endless flux of life,
One will forever circle and replace the other:
Blue skies and rainy days,
Anticipation and regret,
The possible and the impossible,
And that which has never been lacking —
Beauty and sorrow.

1985

Wen Jianliu

(Wen Chien-liu, 1944–76)

A native of Guangdong, Wen grew up in Hong Kong and graduated from the National Zhengzhi University in Taiwan. In 1968 he attended the International Writing Program at the University of Iowa and received an M.F.A. In 1974 he returned to Hong Kong, where he worked as an editor and taught Chinese literature at the University of Hong Kong. He died of cancer.

One poem is written to Guillaume Apollinaire (1880–1918), a French poet of mixed Polish and Italian parentage. A close friend of Picasso, Max Jacob, and Alfred Jarry, among others, and a tireless promoter of the Cubists, Apollinaire coined the term *surrealist* in the introduction to his play *The Breasts of Tiresias* (*Les Mamelles de Tirésias*) in 1917. He died when wounded in the head by shell fragments while serving in the French army.

Wen appended a note to "An Afternoon at the Cemetery": "One day I happened to read the inscriptions on some tombstones. I was struck by the feeling that death might not be the end. All our sorrows, longings, loves, and desires will congeal on the tombstones and, in the eyes of the blind angel, continue to haunt this timeless space after our death. The 'you' in the poem refers to a British air force officer who died in World War II."

SONG

I want to exit this prison of skin and bones
And walk toward the sea's white teeth and the sky's red lips
   A whiff of moist cloud, a swish of blueness
   A bit of mistiness
From who knows how far away, the horses are
Neighing on and on like the wind

   I want to exit this tomb of a room
   And walk where the sheep of light graze on the prairie
A solitary lamp, a white candle
A star here and there
   Roosters crow through the fog
   As the sun rises

I want to walk down this river of a street
And reach the sea of people yonder
   A piece of torn paper, a tiny bit of glass
   The arm of a doll
A junk with black sails is moored to the reef of this world
The ferryman says: "I won't take you across, I won't."

February 11, 1970

AN AFTERNOON AT THE CEMETERY

Many things are still not finished:
An unkept promise,
Some dark desires
That lurk in your decayed heart,

That flick of the eyebrow, the yearning
That has yet to melt. You sorrow like

A dewdrop hidden in a dry well,
Refusing to vanish.

Mosquitoes whisper in your ears, you know.
The place where you lay,
That hole once choked with blood and flesh,
Now gurgles in an April shower.

But there is more than that. Let me say it:
In the shadows of the pines, your long fingernails
Will reach out from under the tombstone and grab
The decrepit afternoon—
Just as her hands and mine try so hard
To hold back the departure of this afternoon.

TO APOLLINAIRE

I, too, can create desolation.
—Mary Shelley

Prologue
Apollinaire, do not fan yesterday, the yesterday of watery clouds
with the wind to your left
let the self-shattering light of tonight's blue moon
jump into the winding brook on my naked back
let the dark blood, the dark blue insanity, murmur
under my skin

Apollinaire, I am galloping
behind me the long street is chasing after my shadow
I am galloping, Apollinaire
the wind's hoofs are faster, wilder, more desperate than time
Apollinaire, you know
I would not lie down
like a ray of light
or a layer of cooled volcanic rock
even if I could return—
a head with no hair, no lips, no beard, no ears,
no eyes, no nose
could neither see nor smell nor kiss nor hear
the green moss loitering by my side

Apollinaire, tell me
how to kick the maelstrom of hunger like a stone
into tomorrow's empty stomach
how to pile up, one upon the other,
all the todays of soured milk
into a crumbling tombstone behind me
like an image, as condensed as the hint of
death in the dewdrops on the low grass by the grave
besides that, Apollinaire
teach me how to arrange, how to
make my poems, like
ants, transport food for Eternity—
decayed grains of rice
like water nourishing the dried gully of the soul

Apollinaire, how I miss
the currents of history, a vista of dark waves
looming like crestfallen, resentful years
do not say: Tragic heroism is a waterfowl
flying toward the edge of the ages
yet unable to find a reed on which to perch—
allow me to remember, remember
my woman: her velvety hair
a swath of night
in the starlight I become the earth
she is a soft
unshelled peanut
in my arms

Apollinaire, let me fall down drunk
in the dirt pile outside tomorrow's door
I don't want to enter
that zone of barrenness I can already glimpse
I don't want to enter
Apollinaire
even if my short-lived dream
is only a gray dove
taking off in the lilac dusk of time
like a pair of startled eyes
but you, who were once dadaist, once surrealist,

once adventurous—
even you could not search
the twists and turns of my soul
because you, Apollinaire,
are already yesterday.

Xi Murong

(Hsi Mu-jung, b. 1947)

Of Mongolian descent, Xi Murong was born in Sichuan and grew up in
Taiwan. She received her B.A. in art from the National Normal Univer-
sity and studied oil painting at the Royal Academy of Art in Brussels.
Her first volume of poetry, published in 1981, went through seven
printings in one year and made her the best-selling poet in the history of
modern Chinese poetry. Currently, she teaches painting in Taiwan. Her
name means "great river" in Mongolian.

The botanical garden of her poem by that name is in Taipei. Among
the works on display in the art museum in the garden are those of the
Shang, or Yin, dynasty, which is well known for its bronze sacrificial
vessels and earthenware. The Xuanwu referred to in the last line is a
famous lake in Nanjing.

BOTANICAL GARDEN

On a July afternoon
After we have seen the Shang bronzes and Yin pottery
We come to the pond full of water lilies.
On a July afternoon

Water-lily pads sway in the wind
Like Mother's dress.
The water lilies carry
The soft scent in the folds of her dress.

But Mother is still unhappy—
Only I know why.
Alas,
My beautiful mother,
How can you not love the lake just because its name is not Xuanwu?

1977

Xi Murong

MUNDANE WORLD

I cannot be
The Buddha sitting on the lotus blossom
I am mundane
My life is in this world of rolling dust
All that belongs to it I covet
Such as happiness and sorrow
The burdens that are mine I shall carry
Though I know that some day
All joys and sorrows will leave me
I will still do my best to collect
Those beautiful, entangling
Memories for which I once lived

September 13, 1979

A PRAYER

I know this world is not all good
I know it has partings and old age
Yet I have only one chance
So, God, please listen to my prayer

Give me a long summer
An immaculate memory
A gentle heart
And a pure love

I can come to this world only once, so
Please give me a beautiful name, too
So that he can call me softly in the night
And, in the light-footed years to come,
Will always remember that once we were in love

November 28, 1979

POETRY'S VALUE

If you ask me abruptly
Why write poetry
Why not do
Something useful

Then I won't know
How to answer you
I am like a goldsmith hammering day and night
Just so I can extend pain
Into a gold ornament as thin as a cicada's wing

I don't know if working so hard
To transform sorrows into
Shimmering words and phrases
Is also
Beautifully worthwhile

January 29, 1980

Luo Qing
(Lo Ch'ing, b. 1948)

Luo Qing is the pen name of Luo Qingzhe. Born in Qingdao in Shandong
Province, he grew up in Taiwan and received his B.A. in English from
the Furen Catholic University in Taipei and his M.A. in comparative
literature from the University of Washington. Currently, he teaches at
the National Taiwan Normal University in Taipei.

   Since the mid-1980s, Luo has advocated Postmodernism in Taiwan; he
coined the term *video poetics* to describe his recent poetry.

SIX WAYS OF EATING A WATERMELON

The Fifth Way: The Genealogy of Watermelons
nobody would mistake a watermelon for a meteor
watermelons and stars are totally unrelated
yet we cannot deny Earth is a star
therefore, we find it hard to deny that watermelons
belong to the lineage of stars
for watermelons and Earth are not only
related as parents and children but also linked
by sibling love, like the love
between the moon and the sun, the sun and us, us and the moon

The Fourth Way: The Origin of Watermelons
obviously, we live on the surface of the Earth
obviously, they live inside
we hustle and bustle, shamelessly
trying to stay out, turning light into darkness
to cover our cold, warmth-seeking selves

they sit in meditation, concentrating
on the inside, molding darkness into physical, composed warmth
in search of growth and self-fulfillment
in the end we cannot escape being driven into the Earth
while they poke and thrust to the outside sooner or later

The Third Way: The Philosophy of Watermelons
the history of watermelon philosophy
is shorter than Earth's, longer than ours
watermelons do not look at, listen to, or say what is improper
they do nothing and have nothing to do with each other
throughout their lives
they do not envy pebbles or despise chicken eggs
neither oviparous nor viviparous
they understand the logic of survival in adversity
therefore, watermelons have no fear of invasions
and even less fear of death

The Second Way: The Territory of Watermelons
if we break a watermelon
it is out of sheer jealousy
breaking a watermelon is the same as breaking a rounded night
the same as knocking down all the stars
or shattering a universe

and the result is, we become even more
jealous, because
the relation between a meteor and a watermelon seed and the friendship
  between a seed and the universe
will reenter our territory
more clearly, more sharply

The First Way: Eat It First

1970

Luo Qing

BREAKING A VASE BY ACCIDENT—
ON HEARING A FRIEND'S DECISION
TO GET A DIVORCE

this morning
I broke a vase by accident
it was a round vase worth all my life savings
when I turned over in my dream
I knocked it with my hand
fresh milk spills and flows out under the door
morning fog seeps in through the window
an antique vase, as old as Neolithic pottery
is broken
into pieces
in my home
but please do not panic
you do not need to feel sadness,
regret, or anger
or try to put it back together again

for, once broken
what was familiar becomes strange
high-powered glue and skilled hands
may bring back its original shape
but without the original spirit
it will fall apart again
it will break again
after it is broken
the whole is still there
just as under the divisions of oceans and valleys
the earth is whole
just as many fragmented and zigzagging lands
make up our countries

though each piece
varies in size and shape
it intimates an entirety
and a brand-new possibility
a complete and self-contained vase
hovers over the pieces
pointing to reconstruction after destruction
so, let them find their new lives on their own

do not force them together
or destroy them completely
let them keep a loose distance
and their broken wholeness
let the whole pieces be remembered
let them glitter

what I am trying to say is
I want to hide the broken starry sky
in my heart
push open the door and walk
in the glorious morning sun
because last night
when I tossed and turned in my sleep
I fell off the bed
and broke all my dreams
because this morning
when I hopped off the bed
I knocked down my only family heirloom
by accident
I broke myself

the broken me
is like a jug of fresh milk
spilling and flowing into the morning fog
to merge with the misty air
to become a clear wind
and enter everyone's breath
so this is how I
walk out the door
leisurely and calmly
please don't mistake me
for the newborn sun at dawn
or the setting sun
at the end of the day

look
I am
walking toward you from the sky
each step a star
I am turning into
the rain of time
to dissolve the earth

Feng Qing

(Feng Ch'ing, b. 1949)

Feng Qing is the pen name of Feng Jinglu. She was born in Ji'nan and grew up in Taiwan, where she received her B.A. in history from the Chinese Culture University. Feng started publishing poetry in 1978.

WHAT WERE YOU DOING THEN?—FOR A.L. ON THE NIGHT BEFORE HIS ENGAGEMENT

Around nightfall
I walked out of your sight
Dejected, I bade you a hurried good-bye
The clouds were strolling
The stream was singing
The trees were doffing their last garments in the breeze
At that moment, what were you doing?

At night
You stuffed yearning into a white envelope
And thought of me sitting on those white stone steps
Of my pretty tip of a nose moist with dewdrops
When the rain from the plantain leaves
Added two new rows of tears for me
What were you doing then?

At night
You pretended to be happy
Yet could not help remembering
How my laughter spilled over and wetted your books
And your favorite lines were probably in my shadow
Do you know
What I was doing by the window?
I dipped my finger in the moonlight
And wrote you a bright letter
What were you doing at that moment?

Feng Qing

ON THE LAKE

Her breathing was a cool pavilion on the water
Surrounded by the color of willow twigs.
A black butterfly, scented, perched on her hair;
The twilight singing on the lake was mysterious.

Will withered flowers regain their charm?
It's like waiting for a swan to die.
Before the moonlight gilded the lawn,
Trembling love was an unfinished game.

How many times were water willows used in conversation?
Her smile was bitter,
Beautiful yet pathetic.
The picking hand shook from the very beginning.

Who hung the stars on the pavilion on the lake
And let the past jingle there?

BRACELET

Things of the world
Are far less translucent
Than the bracelet on your wrist.
You said the color of the bracelet has intensified.
So has autumn.

It has sucked the blood of life
While your beautiful self
In your frequent gaze
Sneaked into
The deepest recess of the mirror.

1980

DWARFS

A sleepless night
Fooled into wakefulness by dwarfs blowing bubbles

I was once grateful
For the dwarfs, as blissful as fairy tales
Who embroidered bright flowers and fruits on my pale sheets

But this is a deciduous winter
The little money in my pocket
Is not enough to buy
A piece of chewing gum.

So I know
Our childhood is gone
(Stolen by dwarfs in uniforms with two rows of buttons)
But purity and maturity have not yet come
As I turn the pages of a fairy tale
I still suffer from a mild seasickness
Those little people who come and go
Are illogical sensualists
They love to whistle
Wipe tear tracks off a clown's face
So I have the more reason to be alone
To practice my chronic stuttering

With a fairy tale and an apple
I climb onto the roof
To see the earth's rosy light fade and the moon rise
Wildflowers spring up along the edge of the sky
I bite into the apple
Then become certain that I am still easily frustrated
And identify with the heart of a child

Jiang He

(b. 1949)

Jiang He, which means "river and stream," is the pen name of Yu Youze. Born in Beijing, Jiang published his first poems in 1980. A major Misty poet, he now lives in New York City.

The following poem depicts Zhang Zhixin, a Communist who, for her criticism of the Party, was jailed and executed during the Cultural Revolution. Her vocal cords were cut before her execution.

Jiang He

AN UNFINISHED POEM

1. An Ancient Tale
I am nailed to the prison wall
Gathering black time—flocks of crows
From every corner of the world, every night in history
Peck at heroes one after another on this wall
Their pain turns into rocks
Lonelier than the mountain
To open and to build
To mold the character of the people
Heroes are crucified
Eroded by the wind, beaten by the rain
Their blurred images on the wall
Their broken limbs and faces
Are flailed by the whip, pecked by the dark
The hands of my ancestors and brothers have worked hard
To pile themselves into the silent wall
Once again I am here
To resist and forestall slavery
To shake the mud off the wall with my fierce death
To make those who die in silence get up and shout

2. Suffering
My daughter is going to be executed
The gun barrel walks toward me—a dark sun
Walks toward me in a parched land
The fingers of sere trees
Spasmodic wrinkles on my face
I suffer from the same calamity as the land
My heart is thrown to the ground
My daughter's blood splashed on the soil
A child's tears flow down my face
They are salty, too
In winter brooklets are frozen
Rivers stop singing
Sister, daughter, wife
Her collar torn, her hair falling down
Tides surge against rocks
My hair is a sea
Father, husband, son

My hands tumble on the sea of hair
Knuckles pop dismally
Ships and forests flourish

3. A Short Lyric
As if in a dream
I became a girl
And entered this world
On a squeaky, pebbled road
On a broken shadow
I ran with bare feet
My blood seeped into
The dew
Drops of red agate sparked on my heaving chest
For a tender green heart
To open at dawn
I dedicated youth's innocent turmoil
And the white bridges of the arms
In my quest for the sun
No longer do I fear the stars shivering in the water
The grove of books, the gropings of the night
I've become a star
No longer trembling

4. On the Way to Execution
A cheating wind covered the window
A slaughter was going on
I could not hide in the house
My blood would not let me
The children of the morning would not let me
I was thrown into jail
Cuffs and shackles bury themselves in my flesh
The whip weaves a web on my body
My voice is cut short
My heart is a fireball burning on my lips
I walk to the execution ground, glancing contemptuously
At this night in history, this corner of the world
There is no other choice—I have chosen the sky
The sky will not rot
I must be executed, or darkness would have no place to hide
I must be born in darkness to create light

I must be executed, or lies would be smashed
I object to everything that light does not tolerate—including silence
All around me are crowds driven here
People who have been deprived of light
I, too, stand among them
To see myself executed
See my blood run dry drop by drop

5. An Unfinished Poem
I am dead
Bullets left holes like empty eye-sockets
I am dead
Not to leave behind a sob, a sigh of being moved
Not so flowers can bloom on the grave
The emotion of my people is rich enough
The prairies are covered with dew every day
The rivers run to the sea every day
Have we not been touched often enough
By this ancient, moist emotion?
I am nailed to the wall
My lapel sways
Like a rising banner

Mang Ke

(b. 1950)

Mang Ke is the pen name of Jiang Shiwei, who was born in Shenyang
and raised in Beijing. In 1969–76 he lived in the countryside near
Beijing and worked on a production team. He started writing poetry in
1971 and founded *Today* with Bei Dao in 1978.

SPRING

The sun gives its blood
To the dying earth.
It sets the sunlight flowing
Into the body of the earth

And makes green leaves and branches
Grow from the bones of the dead.
Can you hear it?
The offshoots of dead bones
Are the clinking winecups of flowers.

SUNFLOWERS IN THE SUN

Do you see
That sunflower in the sun?
Look at it—its head is not lowered
And bends backward.
It's turning its head around
As if to bite off the
Rope around its neck
Held in the hands of the sun.

Do you see it?
Look at the sunflower's lifted head,
Its eyes glaring angrily at the sun.
Its head shines
Even when the sun is covered.

Do you see that sunflower?
You should go near and take a good look.
You will find
Its life is connected to the earth's.
You will feel
The earth beneath its feet.
Pick up a handful—
You can squeeze out blood.

Mang Ke

ONE GROWS OLD EVEN AFTER DEATH

The gray hair of the dead grows from the earth,
Which makes me believe one grows old even after death.

Even after death, nightmares pounce on you;
You still wake up frightened and open your eyes to see

Another day emerging from eggshells
And quickly starting to peck at food on the ground.

You can also hear your own footsteps
And the laughter of your legs; you grieve

And remember, although your head is empty,
Although the people you remember have decomposed.

You can praise them, as well as your lover—
And hold her face with two steady hands,

Lay her down on a haystack,
And watch her clumsily stretch her luscious body.

You know how to wait, too, how to wait for sunlight
Blown away by the wind like a ragged straw mat;

You wait for the sunset, which evades you
The way you evade a ferocious beast,

And you wait for the night when she lets you hold her in your arms,
Docilely lets you caress and ravish her.

Perhaps you can lie down from fatigue and close your eyes
To listen to the beasts howling and fighting in the sky.

And you can worry—perhaps one night
The blood of the sky will gush to the earth;

You can still stand to mourn a dead face,
Whose eyes stare at you;

You can still hope that one lives forever,
That you're not prey

To be roasted and swallowed,
To feel unbearable pain.

Gray hair grows from the earth,
Which makes me believe one grows old even after death.

Duo Duo

(b. 1951)

Duo Duo, which means "much much," is the pen name of Li Shizheng. Born and raised in Beijing, he became close friends with Mang Ke in the late 1960s and later, with Mang, Bei Dao, and others, published *Today*. A newspaper reporter for ten years, he left China on June 4, 1989, after the Tian'anmen Square Massacre, and lived for a year in England, where he taught Chinese at the School of Oriental and African Studies. He now lives in the Netherlands.

His poem "Handicraft" refers to Marina Tsvetayeva (1892–1941), a Russian Symbolist poet who committed suicide under political oppression.

HANDICRAFT—AFTER MARINA TSVETAYEVA

I write the poetry of degenerate youth
(Unchaste poetry)
I write poetry that is ravished by the poet
In a long narrow room
And is tossed in the street by a café
My indifferent
Remorseless poetry
(Herself a story)
My poetry that no one reads
Like the history of a tale
She who has lost her pride
Her love
(My aristocratic poetry)
Will eventually be married off to a peasant
She is my wasted days

1976

IN A FALLOW FIELD IN THE NORTH IS A
PLOW THAT HURTS ME

In a fallow field in the north is a plow that hurts me.
When spring lies down like a horse, from an
Empty carriage for collecting corpses
A head made of stone
Gathers storms of death.

The steel hair of the storm that brushes
Against the hat
Is emptiness—the time after death
Has taken off his face:
A brown beard stretches forward
To gather the dignity long fallow in the north.

Spring is like the bell gnawing at his heart,
Like the sound of a child's head sinking under the water in a well,
Like a child being boiled over a fire.
His pain is like a giant

Sawing lumber
As if sawing his own leg—
A sound weaker than sadness
Threading through the sawmill where work has stopped,
Through the lonely storerooms.
It's the loneliness of a sower walking to the end of the field.

A flax-colored peasant woman
Waves her hand although she has no face,
Waves at the bent back of a plowman.
An improficient mother has no memory,
But she waves—like a stone
From a distant ancestor.

1983

LOOKING OUT FROM DEATH

Looking out from death, you always see
Those whom you shouldn't see
You always pick a burial site at random
Always sniff around, then bury yourself there
Bury yourself in a spot they begrudge you

They shovel dirt onto your face
You should thank them, thank them again

For your eyes will never see the enemy
From the direction of death will come
Their hostile shouting
But you will never hear
That wholly painful cry

1983

LANGUAGE IS MADE IN THE KITCHEN

If language is made in the kitchen,
Then the heart is the bedroom. They say,
If the heart is the bedroom,
Fancy is the master of the bedroom.

In the fancy expressed in a bird's eyes,
A boy who fiddles with a mute
Admits: Chaos
Is exactly like rhythm

A brain that cannot dream
Is but a wasteland of time
The boy who fiddles with the mute admits it
Although he does not understand:

A sterile seed
Does not produce images
Every seed is a reason,
A reason

To be spoken. Not spoken, it is
Just like an address. Without speaking,
The barbarian smoking a cigarette thumbs a walnut
Onto the table. They say

All discussions
Must stop—even though
The horses around us are peacefully
Observing human eyes.

1984

THEY

their hands in their pockets play with coins and their genitals
play with another way of growing up

at the center of the stripper's bent-over hips
is a tiny church moving about on the white horse's three legs

they are watching it with their noses
yet their fingernails will sprout from the earth in May

when the metal tool in heat thrusts at the earth one last time
they will become part of the sacrificial field

the silence that died long before the man did
renders immutable all that they know

so they think stubbornly, they do things
they donate their childhood

to make death complete
they have borrowed our experiences

1991

Shu Ting

(b. 1952)

A native of Fujian, Shu Ting was relocated to the countryside before she
finished junior high school. She published her first poem in 1979 and is
a major Misty poet.

   Goddess Peak, the subject of one poem, is a famous rock shaped like a
woman by the Yangzi River in Sichuan Province. According to legend, it
is the transformation of a woman who stood pining for her absent lover
day after day.

MEMORIES

a knocked-over wine jug
a cobbled street floating in the moonlight
where the green grass is flattened
an azalea is left behind

a eucalyptus grove starts revolving
the stars compose a kaleidoscope

on the rusty anchor
a dizzy sky is reflected in the eyes

a book blocks the candlelight
a finger between the lips
in the crisp, translucent stillness
you dream a half-clear, half-dark dream

DEDICATION

I sympathize with you
By the prow where moonlight floats
On the road where the rain drizzles down
With bent shoulders and hands tucked in your sleeves
As if braving the cold
You hide your thoughts
You do not sense
How my steps slow down
If you were fire
I would be charcoal
I want to comfort you this way
Although I dare not

I salute you
Salute the midnight lamp glowing through your windowpane
Salute you bent over the bookcase
When you tell me about awakening
About how the river overruns
Its banks in spring
You do not ask
How I feel each night
When I walk by your window
If you were a tree
I would be the earth
I want to remind you this way
Although I dare not

Shu Ting

ASSEMBLY LINE

on the assembly line of time
night is nestled with night
we retreat from the assembly line in the factory
and file home
above our heads
an assembly line of stars stretches across the firmament
beside us
dazed young trees stand in a row

the stars must be tired
millennia have passed
their itinerary has never changed
the young trees are sick
smoke and monotony take
their lines and colors
I can feel them
in the rhythm we have in common

what is strange, though
is that I cannot feel
my own being
any more than the trees and the stars
perhaps out of habit
perhaps out of sadness
I no longer have the strength to care
about the fixed position I am in

January–February 1980

GODDESS PEAK

Of the many colored handkerchiefs waving at you
Which one was yanked back
To cover her eyes?
When the people scattered, who
Stood at the stern of the ship,
Her skirt flapping like tumbling clouds?
River tides,
    One high,
        One low.

A sweet dream left sweet sorrow behind.
In heaven, on earth, from generation to generation
Can the heart
Really turn to stone?

Along the riverbanks
A torrent of coneflowers and glossy privet
Instigates a rebellion.
> One would rather have a good cry on a lover's shoulder
> Than be displayed on a precipice for a thousand years.

June 1981

Zhai Yongming

(b. 1952)

Zhai, a native of Sichuan, is considered a poet of the Newborn
Generation. *Woman* is the title of her 1988 poetry collection.

W O M A N

Mother

There are too many places I cannot reach. My feet are hurting. Mother,
  you did not
Teach me how to flush the color of ancient grief in the greedy morning
  light. My heart resembles yours.

You are my mother. I am your blood flowing at dawn;
You are shocked to see yourself in me. You make me wake up

To listen to the sounds of the world. You let me be born, let me be the
  twin sister
Of this terrible world. I can't remember a cry like this one tonight.

The light that impregnated you came from so far away. How suspi-
  ciously, standing between life
And death, you embraced the dark with your eyes and entered the heavy
  shadow under your feet.

In your embrace, I once smiled an enigmatic smile. Who would know
  that
You made me understand everything in a chaste way? But I was not
  touched.

I treat this world like a virgin. Hasn't my hearty laugh
Ignited enough of summer? No?

I was abandoned, all alone in the world, bathed in the
Sad sunlight. When you bend to the world, do you know you have lost
  something?

Time puts me in a mill and lets me watch myself grind to pieces.
Oh, Mother, when I finally become silent, will you be happy then?

Nobody knows how I love you. The secret
Comes from part of you. Like two wounds, my eyes stare at you.

Live in order to live. I seek self-destruction in order to resist eternal love.
A stone is cast away and dries up like bone marrow. Then the world

Has an orphan. All blessings are exposed, but who really knows
That she who stands in her mother's hand will die for having been born.

Let Me Tell You
Why don't you stay put under the tree
And listen to me
Simple, ambiguous, factual—
The usual expression on my face

How wonderful, I am still your little lover
Pampered, gazing at you
With my dry, worried eyes
Knowing how to control myself
Having learned how to smile
Bravely and calmly
While I watch you grab a twig over my head

I don't pretend to be sad
Don't pretend that everything
Is as industrious as love, but who cares?
All kinds of ideas shock me. They come at me
From different directions
They tell me shallowness is paradise
Not much to look at, but that is the best
Of my past
This pure body
Leaning on your arm, I feel the sky is
Descending lower and lower. People slip away from life
With their utilitarian shadows
Who belongs to the future? Or is it something else?

I am not a burden, neither heavy nor strange,
But my profundity is irresistible to you

So the woman says to the man
Loud applause is heard from afar
In the end she is a sexy doll
In the end her beautiful face keeps us here
And joins bodies together
Yet she belongs to no one

1984

Fang Ezhen

(Fang O-jen, b. 1954)

Fang was born in Malaysia and studied Chinese at the National Normal
University in Taiwan. She prefers to romanize her name as Hong Ngoh
Cheng.

EVENING TIDES

The seashore loves evening tides the best
Evening tides no one beholds
Once we were lovers by the shore
We left the human world with affectionate eyes
For the quiet no human can claim
That rolls out from the tides
As they ebb and flow
We saw the moon ripen over the sandy beach
We plucked the moon like a fruit
In the darkness our eyes acquired an absent look
The world was so much like a long train
On the journey we gazed at the rich scenery
But did not know what places we saw
I clung to you
Among the crowded passengers

You held our direction in your arms
We always forgot to look at each other
Ah, my beloved
Among a thousand faces
Will you think of me for once
I was the first lover you held

PARTING

Alas, days always move from morning to night
I live to bring back the hate of lost love
To redeem that complete regret
I wish I would run into you on a strange road
So you could see my beauty
So you could see me with him
So you could see him clasping me close as we walked by
So you could read my latest love poems
So you could regret the treasure you've lost
For the rest of your life

Time flows like a slow autumn river
All the world will know
He and I are perfection
A match made in heaven
Heaven and earth will neither wither nor age for our sake

Time goes by, and my emptiness grows emptier
When will this pain end?
If you return in the next life
Would that I am never born again.

OUT OF TOUCH

At last we are out of touch, at last
The days get cold and the world enlarges
You are the weather of another land
Bringing autumn and winter
At last we are out of touch

I have become temperate
Not in the mood to love

Not in the mood to get angry
I leave fainter footprints
Among ten thousand fair women, I fear to stand out
My pride grows weaker, my temper tamer
Frustrated, I gentle my moods

Besides love
There is only life and then death
Now that love is gone, death is the purpose of living
You are wandering alone
In a strange land
With one new companion after another
As if your love died after I received it
There cannot be a second true love
Suppose "as if" were the truth
Then it was "as if" we parted when we got separated in a crowd

I live in the house of regret
I am too stubborn to change
Like the time I forgot our date
And left you bewildered as you watched my back

There is plenty of lovelessness in the world
The dream that brought us face to face
The adoration of a glance
Make me willing to wait
You are forever drifting
Your final wandering cannot bring you back to love
There is too much twilight
And too much evening
As if the news of our deaths is close at hand—
Sudden news that shakes the waiting lamp
My broken heart is as cold as blood

At last we are out of touch, at last
You are an unreachable dream
Only in my imagination do I cheer up
Seeing you appear in the crowd
But it's only a passerby who looks like you

At last we are out of touch

Liang Xiaobin

(b. 1954)

Born in Shandong, Liang published his first poems in 1979. He lives in Anhui Province.

CHINA, I'VE LOST MY KEY

China, I've lost my key.

That was more than ten years ago.
I ran wildly along the red boulevard;
I ran to the deserted suburbs and shouted in glee.
Then
I lost my key.

The spirit, the spirit of hardship,
Will wander no more.
I'd like to go home,
Open the drawer, and leaf through my childhood album;
I'd also like to see the fresh green clover pressed between the pages.

Besides,
I'd like to open the bookcase door
And take out the *Poems of Heine.*
I want to go on a date
And raise the book in my hand
As a signal of love
Sent to the azure sky.

None of these
Wonderful things
Can be done.
China, I've lost my key.

It is raining again.
Key,
Where are you lying?
I fear storms have corroded you,
You must be all rusty.
No, I don't think so.
I will search obstinately
Hoping to find you again.

Sun,
Have you seen my key?
May your rays
Warm it.

I am walking in a field,
I am searching, following the trail of the heart.
I am pondering
All that was lost.

December 1979–August 1980

SNOW-WHITE WALL

Mama,
I saw the snow-white wall.

In the morning
I went out to buy crayons
And saw a worker
Painting a long wall
Painstakingly.

He turned to me and smiled
And told me
To tell all my little friends
Not to scribble on the wall.

Mama,
I saw the snow-white wall.
Once it was filthy
With many violent words.
Mama, once you cried, too—
Because of the abuse.

Papa is not here anymore,
He is gone forever.

The white wall,
Whiter than the milk I drink,
Keeps appearing in my dreams.
It stands on the horizon
With a spellbinding glow.
I love the snow-white wall.

Never will I scribble on the wall.
Never.
Clear sky as gentle as Mama,
Do you hear me?

Mama,
I saw the snow-white wall.

1980

YOU STILL DON'T HAVE SHOES FOR RAINY DAYS

You still don't have shoes for rainy days
I want to remind you
But am afraid I'll make you worry

I come to see you in the rain
I fold my umbrella, dripping like the wings of a bat
Dripping in your tidy little room
How are you? Why don't you go out to play?
Behind the sheet hanging down the bed
I see many pairs of shoes neatly lined up

You still don't have shoes for rainy days.
You love to cross the lawn strewn with baseball bats and bits of paper
Dew dampens your shoes
The sun visits you from the clear sky
You must have walked many miles
Kicked many rocks
But you still don't have shoes for rainy days
You still don't understand you can't go out when it rains
You still can't step on real mud

Yan Li

(b. 1954)

Born and raised in Beijing, Yan Li started writing poetry in 1974 and
was associated with *Today* from 1978 to 1980. He started painting in
1979 and joined the avant-garde Stars Group, which put on a historical
exhibition in the streets of Beijing on October 1, 1979. In August 1984,
Yan exhibited his avant-garde art in Shanghai, the first exhibition fea-

turing a single artist in the history of the People's Republic of China. In May 1985 he went to study at the Pratt Institute in New York, where he founded the *First Line* poetry quarterly two years later.

GIVE IT BACK TO ME

Please give me back the door with no lock
Please give it back to me even if no room lies behind it
Please give me back the rooster that wakes me up every morning
Please give it back to me even if you have eaten half of it
Please give me back the shepherd's hill song
Please give it back to me even if you have tape-recorded it
Please give me back my relationships with my brothers and sisters
Please give them back to me even if we have only six months together
Please give me back the space of love
Please give it back to me even if you have used it
Please give me back the whole earth
Even if you have divided it into
    A thousand nations
      A hundred million villages
        Please give it back to me

July 29, 1986

QUARTET

With a thud the masters fall,
Spattering their outdated fame all over us.
History stands still at a distance,
Wearing clothes soiled by our aspirations.

With a thump the masters stumble,
Scattering trodden roads all over us.
We dust off the cancerlike names of the roads
And undo buttons like medical terms.

With a splash the masters
Slop the water of grand death all over us.
We peel the skin off posterity
To find their names carved all over the bones.

With a plop the masters
Sit on the bench for kindergarten children
And sprinkle on us the baby smell of the Oedipus complex.
On the floor a choo-choo train rolls toward the future.

1988

GOD'S EXPRESSIONIST MANIFESTO

Crying can express itself only by crying,
By holding our facial expression in its hands
And kneading it in eight directions.
When you wake up and before you go to bed
The mirror fills with the definitions of images;
The puffiness from fatigue or oversleep cannot dodge staring at itself.

History pounds at the door
As if testing your newly fixed ears,
But ambitions require no instruction.
It happens to be lunchtime;
Some time or other every man and woman
Has slipped the sun between two slices of bread,
Because
Hunger can express itself only through hunger.

1989

ALL THE SALTY KNOWLEDGE OF TEARS

He has a criminal record for kissing;
These days his vows are no longer believed.
He also has a criminal record for falling in love;
These days his hate is no longer viewed simplistically.

He cries,
Pouring out all the salty knowledge of tears.
During the day when he cannot go to sleep,
His sheets are tested once again,
For they fail to cover his body.
He cries standing on his feet,
Releasing the humidity of a rainy day.

He has a criminal record for laughing;
These days his crying carries the hopes and dreams of several generations.
He also has a criminal record for crying;
Well, these days his laughter is
Just a disguise for tears
Ready to make a comeback.

1989

Yang Ze

(Yang Tse, b. 1954)

Yang Ze is the pen name of Yang Xianqing. A native of Jiayi in south
Taiwan, he received his B.A. and M.A. in English from the National
Taiwan University and his Ph.D. in comparative literature from Princeton.
He has taught at Brown University and is now editor in chief of the
literary supplement of the *China Times,* a leading newspaper in Taiwan.
   The names of the places mentioned in "On the Island of Bica" were
made up by the poet. The dough sticks, or *youtiao,* mentioned in "In
China" are long sticks made of plain dough that are deep-fried and
served for breakfast, mainly in North China and Taiwan.

SMOKE

Please read me, please read me carefully
I am a palm without lines
I am a face without features
I am a clock without notches or hands
Please read me hard, hard
I am a tombstone without an epitaph or dates

Please read me, please read me carefully
I am not a palm nor a face nor a clock nor a tombstone
But a skinny lowercase *i**
Please read me hard, hard
I am life, I am love, I am the everlasting
Soul, roaring smoke rising from the crematorium
Soliloquizing smoke

1976

*The letter is in English in the original.

Yang Ze

ON THE ISLAND OF BICA

On the island of Bica, Mariann, I saw them
Cover up the brutal memory of the colonizers
With newly built airports and city halls. I saw them
Decorate the square where blood had been shed
With doves and blue ribbons to attract foreign tourists.

On Bica, on the balcony of a hotel,
I met a political exile from Ansasca,
A moderate racist, a fanatic patriot.
"For my country and peace." He raised his glass.
"For love," I mumbled,
Feeling like a cowardly deserter from the Vietnam War.
(Mariann, I am still enamored
Of the moon and your beautiful, anarchist body.)

On Bica, the destination of my emotional journey, Mariann,
I sat down to reflect on ghostly rain in human history—
Times of suffering that I opened the window to search for.
I sat down to reflect on the time before and after us
And the time soon to come, with millions of human heads
Falling to the ground—the image of an abundant harvest.
Mariann, on the merry-go-round,
In the grooves of a spinning record, my poetry—
How would my poetry turn meaningless suffering into meaningful
   sacrifice?
Would my poetry predict only shadows of suffering
And say—love?

1977

IN CHINA

In China, Mariann, I walked down the street on an early morning and
saw people making a charcoal fire in a discarded gasoline barrel; over it
soybean milk was boiling and tasty dough sticks were frying. In China I
walked down the street on an early morning and heard the clamor of a
market, boiling like soybean milk and sizzling like dough sticks.

In China, Mariann, I stood on the street after it rained and waited for
the mourning gowns and white pennants of a funeral procession to pass.
I saw fathers, mothers, brothers, wives and their babies. I saw the family

of the deceased holding bier sashes; other relatives and friends; and curious children running at the rear.

In China, Mariann, I dressed up to attend a neighbor's wedding. I sat up straight at a banquet table temporarily set up on the sidewalk and looked around quietly. The happiness soon caught up with me. Mariann, I'd like to tell you:

This is China, the red character "love" on a gold background, an eternal wedding vow.

December 8, 1977

IN THE WIND

Those who stood in the wind have become the wind.
In the wind at sunset
I am pondering how a poet proves himself.
How does he sing to the robust wind as he leans against it
Except through love,
Through his loved ones, his people,
His time? How does he hold himself in the wind
Like a quivering string, humming
And singing?

Those who stood alone pondering have become the wind.
In the wind at sunset
I am pondering how a man can be freed from anxiety or emptiness.
How can his love be expressed in the sublime
Except through sunlight—
A light harder than marble, a motion more solemn than
Fate across the seasons and the stars? How does he
Stand alone and ponder in the wind when
The setting sun falls into the void without a sound?

Those who stood alone pondering in the wind have become the wind.
In the wind at sunset,
If he sings loudly,
Dead singers will come stand around him,
Like stars revolving in the universe,
To sing about light and love.

If he runs against the wind
At sunset
Crying, the wind
Will run alongside him and wipe away
All the tears.

December 26, 1977

I HAVE SUNG OF LOVE

I have sung of love;
Now I will remain silent.
Joy and sorrow—I have wasted a lifetime
For her.
(Under the tree where travelers rest, I lie with the henceforth-silent lute.)

I have sung of love
And the truths of roses, violets, and tulips,
But for her, for her alone,
I have spent the love of my next life.
(Spring, falling petals, carpe diem.*
Under the tree where travelers rest, I lie with the absent lute.)

I have sung of love;
Now I will be silent forever.
Joy and sorrow—unless
The land sinks to become a sea, the sea
Rises to become a wasteland, the wasteland
Blossoms with roses, and she walks toward me—
Then shall I never come back to life again.
(Spring, fallen petals, carpe diem.
Under the tree where travelers rest, I lie—
With love, which I no longer sing of—as if I were lying in her garden.)

1977

*In Latin in the original, here and below.

Yang Ze

MY HOMELAND IS A MYSTERIOUS RADIO STATION

Standing on the main street in the center of the basin, when
Night falls again, I panic and
Suddenly lose my sense of direction.
Beyond the sound waves jamming the city,
My homeland is a mysterious radio station,
Constantly calling to me
From the corners of the world
With the sound of an evil night,
A savage land.

A Jewish prophet who cherished the glory of his ancient land
Came from Tel Aviv.
He appeared at the New York airport at midnight and shouted:
"Hear,
O Israel!"
I was standing at a street corner among interweaving lights when
Night fell, and I thought I heard
My faraway homeland
Calling the names of her children

From the corners of the world, across
This new, chaotic age.
My homeland once radioed joy
Across the straits—news of the final victory and
The return of the island to the mainland.
Standing on the main street in the center of the basin—
I hear the local accent,
No different from the one my parents heard.

From the corners of the world, through
The atmosphere above the straits,
Voyage sound waves full of toil and sadness, blood and tears,
In the wind, in the explosion in the night.
(The savage land was the only eyewitness and respondent.)
Before they were halfway across,
They turned icy cold.

I am standing on the main street when
Night falls abruptly and tides roar in the straits.
My homeland is a radio station seized by hooligans;

All the staff are killed, and the squawking of bloodstained parrots replaces
The human voices.
I am standing alone on the main street.
"Hear,
O China!"
I thought I heard the desperate cry of the broadcaster dying in a pool of
  blood;
But the crowds and traffic are noisy. It was only
The homeland's regrets,
Lost in the city dust.

1977

LIFE IS NOT WORTH LIVING

Life is not worth living.
A little earlier, maybe
I had a premonition,
A little earlier, before
You—before your pattern, as brilliant and affecting
As a young beast,
Before the papaya tree in the dark,
The ideal balcony, and the starry night,
Before the night of the lovers' magic flute and the unicorn.
When the flute fills the space with its sound,
When it whistles and turns cold at last,
The horn returns to the first
And last dawn on the prairie.

Life is not worth living.
A little earlier I had a premonition.
A little earlier, before my relativism, came
Your absolutism—honest, brave instincts of love and hate
Like a wild rabbit's—and your
Impure temperament
(Which I find so hard to get over):
Inclined to sentimentality, to speed,
And to a little
Indulgence and craziness,
Which come with dreaming.

Life is not worth living.
Much earlier, maybe before books,
Music, and literature,
I had a dim premonition.
Green lights and blue roses,
Marijuana and Zen,
I see you—a woman on a motorbike,
Emulating the headless knight in medieval drawings,
Carrying your long-haired head in your hand,
Galloping toward the prairie at dawn.
When the magic flute whistles again,
It fills the tiny balcony and
Turns cold.
The setting sun over the sea
Is the drug of love and death—
An eternal violence
And craziness.

Life is not worth living. Before the elephants
Gallop on the shore,
Before the sea and the distant skies grow old together,
Ah, young beast who licks its wound,
Only to protect your
First and last sentimentalism
Am I willing to trim a stick into a sword
And be a swordsman undaunted by a thousand defeats;
Like a gopher, I will try hard
To live,
Though before your dreams came
My nihilism, before
Your cave, my light,
Although life is not worth living.

1991

Luo Zhicheng

(Lo Chih-ch'eng, b. 1955)

Luo, who was born in Taiwan, received his B.A. in philosophy from the National Taiwan University and his M.A. in history from the University of Wisconsin-Madison. He is editor in chief of the literary supplement of the *China Times Evening Post* in Taiwan.

"A Book for Babe" is the title poem of a 1989 volume of poetry. In the preface, Luo says the inspiration for the poems came from his "yearning for ideal love, an ideal creative life, and the ideal intellectual and sensual experience," personified in the feminine "Babe." Another poem, "Yelu Apoki," is about a chieftain (r. 907–26) of the Khitans, a tribe originally from the eastern part of Inner Mongolia. Yelu Apoki founded the Khitan state, which became the Liao Empire (916–1218), and named himself emperor. He built walled cities after the Chinese pattern and adopted Chinese institutions extensively—with the help of Chinese ministers, such as the Han Yanhui mentioned in the third stanza.

BODHISATTVA

Gentle Bodhisattva has fallen asleep among sparse candles,
Her pose, a black screen for dreams.
I sneak under her hair to fish;
On every distant star a heavy snow is falling.

A CANDLE FELL ASLEEP IN ITS OWN FLAME

A candle fell asleep in its own flame.
Babe, let's creep down the stairs
To clean up the world you knocked about before you went to bed.
Bring back the tiny anger you left on the carpet
And let it melt in your cozy bed.

A candle fell asleep in its own flame.
Time's cradle rocks,
Death breathes softly;
We'll tiptoe around it,
Babe, with our secret SOS to Eternity.

Let's go fly a kite on the beach.
We'll inquire about the stars' schedule

From the holes poked by meteors in the night sky.
Let's go skiing on your hair.
Please, Everything, do not wake our civilization.

A candle fell asleep, a brush painting wildly in the air as if talking in a
   dream.
Let's go to the bakery before it closes
To buy tomorrow's breakfast.
If you like, afterward
We'll steal the navigation map of Earth.

A candle fell asleep in its own flame.
Babe, blow it out.
The deaths we rear in our bodies grow day by day;
What are they saying to each other? But, Babe,
You are beautiful and tired; the feelings you had
Before you fell asleep lie scattered on the dressing table.

A BOOK FOR BABE

5
I give you permission to lie to me
At least another thousand times—
Who could still hope for corny truths
In the depths of your honest eyes?

58
She said: "I'm sleepy."
Leaning on me, she fell asleep.
I turned the radio off, thinking:
"This is impossible—
How could she be lighter than starlight?"
Because I was thinking this way,
I believed she had fallen asleep
And left me.

1978

Y E L U   A P O K I

Yelu Apoki was even more fiery than his stepbrothers.
With a pull on the bridle, he caught up with
The burning star in one breath—
It fell too fast to make a wish on.
He wrestled ten good warriors with his bare hands
As if dallying with his favorite concubines;
Sometimes he ran headlong into the wind
And poked a big hole in it.

He liked to indulge in food, wine, and sports;
He slapped people's shoulders hard,
Snored when he slept,
Sang, not so competently, when in a good mood.
His greatness covered his flaws;
His flaws did not tarnish his kindness, cunning, or
Insouciance.

He had Han Yanhui emulate Chinese culture;
At the same time, he
Wrote love letters and war declarations in vernacular Khitan:
"The Supreme Emperor under the Sun, your Father, sends His greetings
    to So-and-So"—
His letters always began this way.

He often put his grandchildren and their playmates on his shoulders
And allowed dirty handprints all over
His gold brocade robe;
He tickled
And trained these brawny wolf cubs with laughter.
He always rolled up a map neatly
And peered
Beyond it—and beyond others' visions.
He battled one idea of his with another;
When he sat cogitating in the military tent
Like a survey stake pounded three feet into the ground,
Even Time hesitated to come near,
For the look in his eyes was sharper than an arrow;
Those smitten could only yield and
Shiver.

Yelu Apoki was forgiving—a virtue enjoyed only by
The strong—
But he never relinquished his leather whip, either.
Every day in the north the merciless sandstorm
Clipped the golden fingernails of the setting sun,
Undaunted by the loneliness at the beginning of civilization.
Yelu Apoki led his horse-loving tribespeople
And left deep footprints in
The prematurely wilting history of China,
Including, at times, pillage and slaughter.

"Greatness always contains
Conflict and impurity, which
Lesser personalities cannot bear."
At the head of the troops,
His colors flying,
He boasted to his juniors as he
Marched vigorously in their blood.

January 1984

AESTHETICS

and I
believe anything can happen
as long as I hope
and you
secretly anticipate

this way
we hide in each other's breath
playing hide-and-seek
with those who chide us
and with all that is past
once in a while we are forgotten by virtue
and we
forget ourselves, too

I believe anything can happen
in a flash of the mind
each lightning bolt illuminates a different world
in a flash of the mind

stars squirm like bees
scuffling in lust, thoughts, and long nights
as long as I hope
and you
secretly anticipate
our
reality will be vaster than theirs

August 15, 1984

LOVE POEM

This is going to be a love poem—
A flower doesn't need to feel embarrassed
About its fragrance.

So why don't you come closer?
Hold the firm smile
Of a sigh
And embrace an abundant look.

Say:
"Come here,
  I love you" (I can't think of a substitute).
"Please look after my pride and my wound" (I can't find
  A more sincere gesture than handing them over).
"I'll carry you across the river, on rugged mountain paths;
  I'll carry you across the river back to the village where wild dogs bark.
  Believe me" (what a simple request),
"I'll carry you across the river."

  Say:
"Your expectations are the beginning of my struggle."
  Say:
"Believe me,
  My darling whoever-you-are."

Why don't you come closer?
Your heart is full of grief
Yet fearlessly tender, enraged,
Though it never blames others
To show off its own burden.
When harvesting on sand obscures the direction of seeds sown,

The unpleasant past plays a forgetful musical movement.
In the gay, clamoring crowd,
Why don't you come closer and say softly:
"You're here?
There's not a minute, not a second, when I do not think of you."

Say: "You're not dirty and ugly;
You are my name, my birthright"
(Thus deepening the meaning of my glory and my humiliation).
Say: "You are a sickly, unsightly invalid.
But how could I blame you?
You were my ancestor;
Now you are us."

Or say: "How can I not blame you—yours is not even my name,
But you have been my incurable heartache."
Say whatever you will.

Why don't you come closer, bend over,
Open your eyes wide,
Caress my frailty, my ulcer,
And read the sweat and blood stains on our trail?
Why aren't you angry at infuriating, pitiable stupidity?
Why don't you get upset over the ostentatious, bewildered present?
Those who are awake must endure
The nightmares of
Those who are asleep.

Why don't you come closer?

Say:
"Wait for me. Be patient.
Give me another day or a thousand years.
I will return to the ranks to struggle
And live;
I will think more, dress more nicely.
As long as I do not forsake myself,
I will never be away from you,
My lasting, most endearing idealism."

And if you entrust your tired body to me, I will tend to you
Every time you turn around.

Why don't you stand up,
Put your hand on my shoulder,
And say:

"Come,
Let us—"
(I am getting excited; when we become us,
Cloudy skies suddenly clear up.)
The direction? One stride, and there it is.
As long as you are near me,
My love,
As soon as you ask,
Will I not give it to you?

July 7, 1986

Wang Xiaolong

(b. 1955)

Born on Hainan, Wang is now the general manager of a video company in Shanghai. He is considered a poet of the Newborn Generation.

IN MEMORIAM—DEDICATED TO MY FATHER

1

a bunch of winecups stand on the dining table
one must be yours
I knocked against a drawer
out came the letter you forgot to mail
that pair of old shoes is moored under the dry bed
thinking hard
the razor keeps a few hairs of your rusty beard
why did everything become the past so quickly
when I blow out the match
I raise my head and there you are
smoking in the mirror
every morning you sat there
feeling bored
you were smart
therefore you were incompetent

every time you got mad you were actually scolding yourself
your skin was dark
and had large pores
when a sad flock of wild geese brushed past your eyes
autumn was gone
I am you

2

no, no, you forgot   you
always pushed me out the door
when I thought the matter had blown over
you stood waiting at the street corner as if to punish me
you purposely paid no attention
to the poems on the coffee table
you flicked the cigarette a few times   I think
I was probably that worn aluminum ashtray
that you burned brutally again and again
the moment you turned the lights off it was dark   after dark
you let me run naked in a crowd
and fall from the roof to the sea
I believe this   I believe
now you are beating the back of my head with a disgusted look
all the reason lies in that
I am you

3

if I decided to become a good student the next day
the alarm clock would surely stop in the middle of the night
I wanted to be an honest worker to make money
who would know the next day I would be sent to conduct a chorus
I wanted to be a good husband
but the sausages were always sold out
I don't know why this world
is always at odds with me
I'd rather be a bastard
so I wanted to make up with the world
make up with you
yet you suddenly turned around and left

anyway it is normal to rain on a sunny afternoon
see the raindrops glistening in the sun
as harmonious as a couple of vagabonds
so don't take things too seriously
don't you think so? why don't you speak? you are
such a quiet palm tree

TAXIS ALWAYS COME AT MOMENTS OF DESPAIR

it was like this last time
to go to the restaurant to get married
she and I stood on the roadside
like colorful cotton dolls
acting happy
but sweating like hell in our hearts
hoping the watch was a quarter too fast
did we have the right address?
we didn't know if it would come from the north or the south
so each watched one side of the street
imagining ourselves to be characters in a spy movie
another quarter passed
their faces must be turning green in the restaurant
they are relatives now whether they know each other or not
they struggled for things to say
frequently yelled at the children to stop rehearsing toasts
only when we got there did I remember
the tie in my pocket
I put it around my neck like a belt
no, I'm not committing suicide
this time it is
she, carrying her teeth, medicine, and dirty laundry
like a convict on parole
I count the feet walking in and out of the hospital
trying to figure out
if there are more men or more women in China
I may as well quit waiting
it will surely appear at that moment
that destined moment

Wang Xiaoni

(b. 1955)

A native of Changchun in northeast China, Wang was relocated to the countryside with her family in 1969 and returned to her hometown in 1972. In 1978 she entered the Chinese Department at Jilin University; later she worked at the Changchun Film Studio. In 1985 she moved to Shenzhen in Guangdong Province. She is considered a Misty poet, although her recent work, of which the last poem is an example, is closer to the poetry of the Newborn Generation in its focus on the female psyche.

IMPRESSIONS

I Feel the Sunlight
In the long corridor
I walk

—Facing me is a dazzling window
On both sides is a light-reflecting wall
Sunlight, me
I am standing together with sunlight

—Ah, the sunlight is so strong
So warm that it makes me pause in my steps
So bright that it makes me stop breathing

The sunlight of the whole universe is gathered here
—I don't know what else exists
Only me against the sunlight
Standing here for ten seconds
Ten seconds—longer than a quarter-century

At last I rush down the stairs, push open the door
And run in the sunlight of spring

HOLIDAY, LAKESIDE, REVERIE

By the lake the wind is gusty.
Perhaps I should not have put on a skirt.
Why does the wind make it flap?

If there were no people here,
How free I would be,
Leaving my hair, my skirt, to the will of the wind.

No, I will walk through the crowd nonchalantly.
Why should I be afraid
Of those eyes before and behind me?

1983

HALF OF ME IS ACHING

a pretty little bug
would rather gnaw at my tooth

the right side of the world
suddenly becomes enchanting
the body is a shabby house
from the very beginning

in half of me a black flame is leaping
half of me is filled with the sound of medicine

you reach out both hands
one grabs me
the other grabs the opaque air
pain is life, too
we can never hold it down

sit, then stand up
let the wind blow here and there
when pain sparkles
you realize the world is far from ordinary
we are not healthy
but
we still like to walk around

I use the half that's not aching
to adore you
use my left hand to push the door open
the right side of the world

is bright and luminous
the long hair of pain
floats into a forest
that is me, too
that is another good woman

May 1988

Xiang Yang
(Hsiang Yang, b. 1955)

Xiang Yang, which means "facing the sun," is the pen name of Lin Qiyang. Lin, a native of Nantou in central Taiwan, graduated from the Chinese Culture University and is now editor in chief of the *Independence Evening Post*. He founded the Gathering of Sunshine Poetry Club in the winter of 1979.

The Ba River, the subject of one of his poems, is a river in Chang'an, the ancient capital of China. It is a custom, probably dating from the Han dynasty (206 B.C.–A.D. 220), to bid farewell by the river, breaking off a willow twig to symbolize regret. The word for willow is homonymous with the verb "to stay".

BY THE BA RIVER

To finish this cup of
Green Bamboo Leaf wine is to
Put on a
Green gown of bamboo leaves.

So the legend goes: every year
The color of the willows means the grief of parting.
We are in fact
Migratory birds on the wing. Coming from the south

Or returning to the north, we carry
Moonlight, pressing
A shallow stream into
A moist look in the eye.

Our longing spreads over a range of hills
Like a comma and a period. Between

The exclamation of the rain and the question of the wind
We write down our precocious love

And the beauty of sad nightfall.
For we are the solitary lamps
Standing in the night;
The quest of the moths by the riverbank

And the glow of light
Will be passed on.
Each year at our reunion
We fly and gather.

A union of lamps, too.
Even the roc spreads its wings
To cover the distant land;
Our hands are its skyward flight.

With our totem, green bamboo leaves,
We go forward;
With our vow, a lone spiral of smoke,
How do we burn spring as we go forward?

February 10, 1976

AUTUMN VERSE

Unable to hang on to the somber branches,
Leaves run one by one to the lake's chilly heart of early morning.
Someone walks by the dewy lakeside with an umbrella,
Hears a pinecone jumping down in the woods to his right
And exclaiming:

"So you've come this way?" Ripples
And echoes linger on the shimmering water.
Duckweed stands up abruptly,
Leaving the crisp reflection of the mountain kissing
The azure sky after the rain. And autumn is deeper, much deeper.

November 27, 1979

Yang Lian

(b. 1955)

Yang Lian was born in Bern, Switzerland, and returned to China with
his parents when he was one year old. He started writing poetry when
he was relocated to the countryside near Beijing in 1974–77. Yang par-
ticipated in the Democracy Movement of 1979 and was introduced to
the *Today* group by Gu Cheng. A major Misty poet, he now lives in
New Zealand.

His poem "Dunhuang" is about the stone caves in west China con-
taining Buddhist sculptures and wall paintings from as early as the
fourth century. There are 492 caves. Depicted in one wall painting is an
apsara, or celestial fairy. An apsara entertains the Buddha with music
and sprinkles flowers from her flowing sleeves.

BLUE FANTASIA

Shadows of the sun lie on the waves,
Shaking the palm leaves and the green light.
Dawn comes running to me, placing
White doves on each reef. It is there
That night strikes flying seagulls down. The cliffs rock
And mutter dark echoes. It is there
That cold phosphorous glows and sways.
The boisterous day is dead.

My dream floats among trembling water weeds.
On the bosom of the sky and the sea
Are thousands of violets,
A fragrant world evoking another world,
But it is there that my wet footprints on the beach
Are erased by the tides. It is there
That summer storms blast away as if crazed
And numerous memories congeal in pale hail light.
It is there that maidens walk out of golden seashells
And sing under the cool moonlight.
The sky is fair, the sea calm,
But the last stars of autumn
Glitter alone; the moon
Like a round August orange

Drops into the abyss of my heart. It is there
That rings of dew are shattered.

But where are the crystal grapes under the eaves?
Where are fancies like snow-capped mountains and innocence on the
  grass?
It is there that the carcass of a small boat
Carries the distant storm.
Its sail was like a child
Who once played and shouted in the sea foam.
It is there that time chimes in old age
And dreams drift off like falling leaves.

The sky is fair, the sea calm.
Look, there on the high rocky shore
My white birch is silent
Like a mast that no longer moves;
The world's colors shift under its foot.
It is there, between fleeting moments,
That it does not thank the sunshine or sing with the grieving cicadas
  anymore.
Only growth proves its own destiny.

DUNHUANG

A Flying Apsara
I'm not a bird when the sky disintegrates
I'm not a fish in a dark sea
My body trapped in a certain moment, a certain spot
Am I flying, or am I motionless?
Am I transcending life or struggling on the brink of death,
Rising or falling (in the same elegant posture),
Heading toward millennia to come or millennia past?
My history is this cold wet wall—
My birthday and my last day. I cry all night long
The anesthetic saltiness of the desert fills
This speechless woman
On a tiny piece of pure land; she is as bewildered as chastity,
Fading stars, the mystery of the East.

Flowers are about to fall.
They act with the expected gentleness.

Awake or about to sleep? My slightly open eyes
Extend to the end of infinite time, seeing through nightmares,
A habit of playing the zither in anticipation,
A smile, long rusted, that cannot be wiped off.
Moss is like another decaying wall painting.
I resent darkness yet cannot but follow it.
Night falls—night, the whole world.
The hand of reality clutches the luminous wound of the imagination.

Here singing
Is the specialty of robust young flies.
Throngs of people flow by. I am looked at by those I's.
Under my feet, over my head, are a thousand faces—
All that cannot change the immovable loneliness,
Immense body, and finely wrought emptiness of the cave.
Birth or death—I am a dancing soul
Suspended between heaven and earth, hammered into a thin sheet
On this spot, at this moment, everywhere, through eternity.

Hanging too long, my ribbon has lost its depth;
Too long, the stretch of yellow earth before and behind me.
I sprout, converse with the remains of maidens
In a language that blackens in the tombs,
Or touch them, and they me, with a shivering solitude.

I long to fly in no direction, therefore all directions;
I long to fly around yet retreat to the heartless stillness.
Drifting
In the millennia to come, the millennia past,
I fly like a bird, beyond vision and hearing.
I fall like a fish, with an open mouth yet without a sound.

1982–84

THE STREET OUTSIDE MY WINDOW

It never rains on the street outside my window.
As quiet as a comb,
It sits by my windowsill,
Waiting for a silent woman
Like a tired gull flying from the sea
Or a stone hugging itself.

In the worn gray pack on her back,
A lemon is changing shape.

The street outside my window is covered with snow.
All winter long, I have seen only
Seven stray cats and a man sleeping in a run-down car—
Eight identical pairs of eyes,
Ungrudging like threshed wheat grains.
Their intimacy makes me believe
They have promised to feed each other with their corpses
And guaranteed their gentlest touch.

1991

Gu Cheng

(b. 1956)

A native of Beijing, Gu was relocated to north Shangdong at the age
of twelve to raise pigs with his father, Gu Gong, also a poet. He returned
to Beijing in 1974 and worked as a carpenter. His first poetry was
published in 1977. Gu, who is considered a major Misty poet, now lives
in New Zealand.

FEELING

the sky is gray
the road is gray
the buildings are gray
the rain is gray

in the dead grayness
two children are walking
one in bright red
the other in pale green

THE SQUARE OF A TWELVE-YEAR-OLD

I like to wear
Old clothes
And walk through the square
As the morning spreads out

Clumps of wild grass in the suburbs
Explode soundlessly
In the crannies
I cannot stay
Those skinny black crickets
Have started singing

I am only twelve years old
I lower my eyes
The few grown-ups who get up early
Won't pay attention
To the thoughts
Of a child in old clothes
Besides, birds have started singing
In the distance the nose of a motor is congested
Which is enough to make a few people
Happy or sad

Who could know that
In my dreams
My hair has turned gray
I have reached the age of fifty
Have examined the whole world
I know everything about you—
The night and the lamp just turned on
Your dark blue fatigue
Your experiences
While you stayed the same through thick and thin

I hope I am good-looking
I hope no one will
See me in my old clothes
The blowing wind
Presses them against my body
I cannot cry out
I can only walk as fast as I can
Just like this
Walking through the twelve-year-old square
Overgrown with wild grass

August 1981

THE END

In the wink of an eye
The avalanche stopped
On the riverbank, giants' skulls piled high

The junk in mourning clothes
Slowly passes by
Spreading a yellowed shroud behind it

Many handsome green trees
Their trunks twisted in pain
Are consoling the brave with tears

God has buried the hacked moon
In thick fog
All has come to an end

The gloomy contours of the hills
Represent a vague history
Still being recorded

ACCOMPLICE

you are always watching the world outside
your feet are looking for slippers
you are married
and own a rye field
you stole in your dreams

you take another look at the steps outside

NARRATIVE

three men ran away from the battlefield

they used leaves to mix drinks, gave away their bullets at night, walked
  through town fairs where satin banners fluttered

then the military police came

he was the last one dragged across the square
dark hair like a dream
dark hair like a dream covering his eyes

EXPECTED MISFORTUNE

expected misfortune
did not crush
the man talking in front of the sad troops

the flags dragging at their feet

their eyes were layered dream-shadows
all elephants ran toward the church

violent acts
of clothes, tongues, fresh flowers

people always wept like cowards
trees stretching all the way from the empty lot to the seashore

Xia Yu

(Hsia Yu, b. 1956)

Xia Yu, who also writes under the name Tong Dalong, studied film and
drama at the National Institute of Art in Taiwan. In addition to poetry,
she writes essays, song lyrics, and stage scripts. She lives in France.

The epigraph to the poem "Jiang Yuan" is from Song 245 in the *Book
of Songs,* the earliest anthology of Chinese poetry. Jiang Yuan was the
mother of the legendary ancestor of the Zhou people—Hou Ji, the god
of millet. In "Heavy Metal" the poet sometimes uses the third-person-
plural pronoun for "them" and "they" with an animal radical in the
character, rather than a man or woman radical. In the translation,
quotation marks set off the pronouns written with the animal radical.

ARCHEOLOGY

1

the dragon degenerated into a man
obviously it was a man
a mammal
walking, peeing in an upright position
good at analysis
ticklish
foresighted

he rarely visits brothels
or he would have to brush his teeth
and wash his face
at times he uses a fake military ID
and puts on a stern look

gregarious
a picky eater
his right ear is slightly larger

2
some evidence is hidden in the pocket
pieces of eggshells
sticky
it's early winter
the coat has a moldy smell
I can't help being confused
about my genealogical hunt

3
"I finally believe in gravity"
he sits in a dim corner
with his glasses on
his wool sweater smells of camphor
because he is sad
therefore he is proud
"except for an impressive family lineage,
I have nothing"
except for all the plights of men:
ulcers, hemorrhoids, real estate
"the glory that was Greece, and the grandeur that was Rome"
nuclear bombs
I analyze his spinal cord
investigate his jaw
and dental structure and fall in love with him:
"it's incredible
perfect evolution!"
"surely," he says
"it must be an oversight of the Creator"

1982

Xia Yu

CRIME OF PASSION

I was afraid
that I'd suddenly die
while I was secretly writing your name
then
the world would discover what they weren't supposed to know

and think that was the last word
and that they were the ones
who knew best

I was merely writing your name
in order to erase it
but I'm afraid
it's too late
for everything has taken place

when it did
you stubbed out the cigarette
stood up from the depressed couch
wearing your grayish blue shirt
with its lazy wrinkles
and you walked in the street
leisurely
leisurely

the red light blinked on
you halted—
grayish blue
was already reaching the limit of blueness
which I loved deeply
and liked

1982

Xia Yu

COMMON KNOWLEDGE

a woman
bleeds once
a month

understands the snake's language
is good at ambush
is not prone to keep appointments

1982

JIANG YUAN

She who gave birth to the first people
Was Jiang Yuan.
How did she give birth to the people?
She sacrificed and prayed.

whenever it rains
I feel
like copulating, propagating
descendants, spreading them
all over the world, with their own
    dialects
        clans
kingdoms

like a beast
in a hidden cave
whenever it rains

like a beast
using the human way

1983

Xia Yu

MAKING SENTENCES

I Cannot But
I cannot but
leave footprints
humbly, kindly
on their
wet cement
hearts

Then
then I walked away
leaving behind these dirty words:
"I love you"

Whenever
whenever there is a moment like this
I feel music rising
dissolving the metaphor in progress
and circuitous
gentle
individualism

After . . . Before . . .
my thought after I wake up
before I brush my teeth:
"forever"
the most heartbreaking word
I've ever heard

1983

A CAN OF FISH

Lying in the tomato sauce
The fish may not be happy
The sea does not know that

The sea is too deep
The shores do not know that, either

This story is crimson
Besides, it is corny
So it is actually about tomato sauce

1984

HEAVY METAL

Imagine men carrying "them," walking
running into friends on the street
maybe men are jealous of each other, but "they" are not
men compare themselves with each other
no, women do not talk about "them" a lot
women are proud only of their soft empty holes
when "they" in women's hidden places
bear witness to the frailty of steel
in addition to giving women pleasure
women imagine men carrying "them," walking
running into friends on the street
"they" are jealous of each other
but men are not

1985

VENTRILOQUY

I walked into the wrong room
and missed my own wedding
through the only chink on the wall I saw
all proceeding perfectly: he wearing a white blazer
she with flowers in her hand, the ceremony
vows, kisses
with my back toward it: fate is the ventriloquy I worked so hard on
   (the tongue, a warm-blooded water creature
   in a small aquarium, squirming tamely)
the creature said: yes, I do

1986

Liu Kexiang

(Liu K'e-hsiang, b. 1957)

Born in Taizhong in central Taiwan, Liu received his B.A. in journalism
from the Chinese Culture University and is now assistant editor in chief
of the literary supplement of the *China Times*.

 His poem "Bristle Grass" is about the February Twenty-eighth Incident
of 1947, when an inspector in the government-run Liquor and Tobacco
Bureau beat up an illegal tobacco seller and shot an innocent bystander.
The incident led to a series of conflicts between the Nationalist govern-
ment and native Taiwanese dissatisfied with its high-handed rule in
which many Taiwanese were arrested and killed. The incident was a
taboo subject until the mid-1980s.

BRISTLE GRASS

February, the end of winter, the cold rains not yet over
That night no one dared leave home
It was Uncle Tu and others in the village who went to the square
They carried you away with tears in their eyes
There were so many bodies; they weren't sure if those were you
Under the starlight they groped along the road
Stealthily they returned to Crow Stream among the rushes and pebbles
They dug more than ten holes
To the distant howling of wild dogs
They prayed that you sleep in peace

Every year bristle grass grows tall on your graves
I arrive with a sickle and my son, who is already in elementary school
If you were alive, your children would be this big
He always asks me why I come here every year
I'm worried that he'll know when he's grown up
As usual I leave a bouquet of white chrysanthemums for you
I never know what to say
The past lingers in my mind
That day you said I was a scholar, that I shouldn't go
You left and no one came back

February, the end of winter, when the north wind gusts
My son whines about going home
I am taking him home now
Every time the bristle grass rustles behind me
A Xiong, A Xin,
I feel like turning around
To see if it is you coming back

CHOICE

This is an age of anxiety
Rebellion and escape are likely to occur
Once I gave up my job
And traveled alone on the west coast
Observing waterfowl
I drifted from one seashore to another
I did not meet any friends of my age
Just saw schoolchildren picnicking
Or once in a while, old men fishing by the sea

Tonight, as in former journeys
I am leaving the city
I want to come back, to imitate the silent crowd
As long as I engage in work that stays away from politics
What I most fear is to
Castigate the ruling power, as I did before
And then, like a young rebel wandering
In search of truth,
Switch from one political magazine to another
Over an ideological conflict

A few days ago, when I passed through the far south
An old classmate from college hugged me
And introduced me to his wife
His child called me uncle
That night, like now, I could not sleep
It is a worrisome, complicated life
I am thirty years old, single

And flutter with the cataclysmic changes of the times
I can forget them only by traveling

Tonight I continue to feel exhausted
I would like
To settle down in a border town
Yet how reluctant I am

GRANARY MEMORIES

Maybe you know who slept in the granary
Early in the morning, I left, tracking the wild strawberries along the
  dam
Rice stalks lay scattered in the hedges

I followed a group of mountain climbers
To Pinecone Forest and sat down
At dusk. When wild smoke drifted from the ravine
I could feel them turning around, reaching toward
The dewy prairie, forgetting their fatigue
Yes, they must have cut enough pine branches
To make a late-autumn camp fire; yes
In the beautiful Grass Mountain night
They must be falling fast asleep

With a blanket over me, I lean on wet, rotten logs. Now I recall
You went into the granary and gathered kindling
Smoke from a cook fire was rising, and roosters were crowing
Maybe it was raining, too

Early morning in the ravine
Is so cold. I walk through the forest in fog and rain
And proceed along the stream

1978

DESCENDANTS OF MYTHS

they invented myths
myths transformed them

mammals with dignity
strictly territorial hunters

advanced in their social organization
not at all hirsute, on a mixed diet
with a strong sexual drive
they once lived in jungles
polite, they know how to smile
but resent strangers

they can kill each other from a distance
from a longer and longer distance

Chen Kehua

(Ch'en K'e-hua, b. 1961)

Chen was born in Hualian in east Taiwan. He received his M.D. from the National Taipei Medical School and is an ophthalmologist at the Veterans Hospital. He has published three volumes of poetry since the early 1980s, as well as prose, television scripts, and song lyrics.

   "A Reply—To Gu Cheng" is a sympathetic response to Gu's poetry, much of which deals with the suffering and the fantasy worlds of innocent children. Gu's "I Am an Impetuous Child" contains these lines: "I have only me / my fingers and my wound."

WHERE LIFE TURNED

At the intersection I stopped and waited for you
Hoping you would come up and inquire
I would tell you softly
This is where my life turns

For a long time now, my dream
Surfaced in shop windows at dusk
You were running; I was following
Picking up the jewels you cast on the road
And throwing them into the riptide

The moon rose over the sea
A cloud, filled with moonlight, descended, sprinkling silver raindrops
You pointed at them, panting: Once a child got lost there
So he did. I thought: It was the tides of your sighs
That wiped away his footprints

So we said good-bye to each other in silence
As if you were a bright neon light
In a boisterous downtown alley. In silence
I insisted, yet I didn't tell you
That once I waited for you where my life turned.

INTERIOR DESIGN

Bed
two big dreams lie side by side, rotund and neat
a distance apart
they do not interfere with each other

each night it is ruffled—two heads lying side by side
do not ask
where the sperm and tears that have no place to go
actually go
each night
they dream of a bright ripe womb
where sperm and eggs
are stranded without a sound

A REPLY—TO GU CHENG

Are you in pain? How painful is it? Can you bear it? This pain—
I cannot find the wound anywhere.
My footsteps disturbed the tiny herbal garden as
I picked the wild ginger and the pinks that sprouted last night.
Late on the day before a long journey, when the scampering crows were
    tired,
You calculated the calmness and storminess in your luggage;
Your eyes evaded tears, your will warded off time:
"Let me first find a prairie that winter will never invade
  Where you can settle with the lambs of poetry that you rear."
Who will give an excuse and put an end
To that hope that will never heal,
Put an end to the soul's bleak imagination and dreary waiting?

In the end you did not remind
This shadowy world of its forgotten promise to a firefly.
Let those who thirst for sleep receive a bed and the embrace of a dream;
Let those going forward receive a torch; those who fall, a kiss.
Let those who long to fly have wings and a distant destination;
Let those in pain have a reply.

WHY ARE THERE STILL LOVE POEMS?

Why are there still love poems? I have loved completely,
Have been complacent,
And have broken apart.
What does youth have to do with me now?
My luggage is simple,
My residence well lit, my only neighbor
A diligent student at an evening school.
Why are there still love poems?

I have died before (died completely),
Have made an effort
To shake myself up,
And have been humble. Now my blood is calm,
My head is at a moderate temperature,
My limbs are flexible,
My vision is wide (so are my blind spots).
No longer do I detect my heartbeats easily
Or the few dreams I have.

Why are there still love poems?
The gray, misty city allows no trace of mystery;
Bright clear lust allows no hint of poetry.
I have renounced it
And regretted renouncing it. As to my overly uneventful age of twenty,
As to human nature,
How relaxed I am now.
Why, why are there still love poems?

Lin Yaode

(Lin Yao-te, b. 1962)

Born of parents from Fujian Province, Lin graduated from the law school of the Furen Catholic University in Taipei. He is a prolific writer of short stories, novels, and literary criticism, as well as poetry. Like Luo Qing, Lin is an advocate of Postmodernism in Taiwan.

Lines 16–18 in "Images of Nonbeing" are quoted from *The Way and Its Power* (*Daodejing*), a Daoist philosophical text attributed to Laozi (sixth? century B.C.).

IMAGES OF NONBEING

A porcelain cup on the desk,
A flute hanging on the wall,
A car wheel leaning against the closet.

Early in the morning I wake up startled.
A vast emptiness, faster than light,
Envelopes the ant-paced words of my thoughts.
A vast emptiness
Spills from the holes of the hub, the flute, and the cup,
Images of a nonbeing that has never left history.

A nostalgia
Older than the universe and time,
Mocking at humans, who are bound by language,
Raises its head among the words.
Images of "   "—silent, hidden, discreet—
"You look but do not see it;
You listen but do not hear it;
You grab but do not touch it."
A soundless music,
Never taken over by substance and desire,
Trickles from the holes of the hub, the flute, the cup.

1986

Lin Yaode

FIN DE SIÈCLE—ILLUSTRATION FIVE OF REPORTAGE POETICS

If I marry my heart to the snow in the distant north,
Will I bring you happiness?
I can only peel my shadow off the back of the chair
And let it dry on the balcony railing.
I wonder if we will have another day like today?
How pleasant is
The sunshine!

By the way, that night
When you pushed open
The window,
Pushed open the night
To let light in and darkness out,
The planets were going in circles,
The universe was moving, alive,
Moving.
The Hunter raised his heavy bow,
The Crab rolled its eyeballs,
The planets
Revolved around a million mornings and midnights.
"How mysterious," you said.
"Yes,
When the imaginary bell of peace rings in the universe,
A planet
Will explode quietly
Before it can hear
The sound of weeping," I replied.

This is a magnificent or not-so-magnificent farewell.
In City K the antinuclear demonstrators walk through
Your nights and my mornings
With pictures of smiling babies.
Their hands are not sore, and none complains of fatigue,
Although by tomorrow noon, when the nuclear explosion occurs,
Their footprints will have dried.

I wonder if I can bring you happiness.
I wonder if we will have another day like today.

1986

1 9 9 0

The backs of the breaking waves are circuit boards from antiquity,
Their gigantic skeletons covered with crystalline chips.
The world looks so magnificent
It is about to break out of my skull,
And I have no way to stop
Those grinning angels and their gospel.

January 1, 1990

Chen Feiwen

(Ch'en Fei-wen, b. 1963)

A native of Taizhong in central Taiwan, Chen received a B.A. in creative
writing from the Chinese Culture University. She is now editor in chief
of the children's section of the *Independence Morning Post*.

In her poem "Notes on Fleas on a Cat" she refers to the initiation
marks on the head of a newly ordained nun. Buddhist acolytes, like
nuns and monks, are bald; upon taking final vows, a number of
scorchmarks are made on the scalp with a lighted incense stick.

GARDEN EARTH

To make you believe
That we can have
A "Garden Earth"
Please forgive me
For not letting you pluck flowers.

Can you not
Imagine yourself a flower,
One that
Sleeps embraced by moonlight each night
In a gentle stream of tiny dreams?
Wouldn't that be wonderful?
The kiss of dew would awake you;
You would yawn and yawn
While you freshened up in the wind.
Now and then I would pass by and greet you.

Can I not
Forbid you to pluck flowers
For the sake of that delightful greeting?

If we wander all over the world
When in fact we are
Strolling in a garden,
Isn't that wonderful?
We pass by the home of every flower,
Bend to greet them,
And, with a smile, become flowers, too.

To bring about
Our "Garden Earth" sooner,
I have smashed ninety-nine vases
And antagonized the flower vendors of the entire street,
Yet you walked away with an armful of flowers.
Sitting dejectedly in your fragrant shadow
I say again and again with tear-filled eyes:
Do not pluck flowers.

1983

NOTES ON FLEAS ON A CAT

Flea 3

Finally, my dog has reached puberty. He holds onto my leg and makes
love to it—his movement is both natural and correct. I give him a kick
and recall the frustrated, bewildered look on the face of a boy I humili-
ated when I was sixteen when he made an immoderate request for love.

Flea 7

On a crowded bus, my chin almost perches on the bald head of a young
nun. I stare at it. A shaft of rosy light refracted through the window
strikes her head, which has yet to receive initiation marks. Like an
ancient bronze mirror radiating an eerie light, it reflects my fast-
growing, fast-decaying senses and desires.

Flea 9

Those adults stuck a fish bone in my throat to help me remember the
fear and the pain whenever I can't help saying "love." Maybe they were
right, but I hate them.

1988

Select Bibliography

Translations and Critical Studies of Individual Poets

Ai Qing. *Selected Poems of Ai Qing*. Ed. Eugene Eoyang. Bloomington: Indiana University Press, 1982.

Bei Dao. *The August Sleepwalker*. Trans. Bonnie S. McDougall. London: Anvil, 1988.

————. *Old Snow*. Trans. Bonnie S. McDougall and Chen Maiping. New York: New Directions, 1991.

Chang, Shiang-hua. *Sleepless Green Green Grass and Sixty-Eight Other Poems*. Trans. Stephen L. Smith. Hong Kong: Joint Publishing Co., 1986.

Cheung, Dominic. *Feng Chih*. Boston: Twayne, 1979.

Duoduo [Duo Duo]. *Looking Out from Death: From the Cultural Revolution to Tiananmen Square*. Trans. Gregory Lee and John Cayley. London: Bloomsbury, 1989.

Gu Cheng. *Selected Poems*. Ed. Seán Golden and Chu Chiyu. Hong Kong: Chinese University Press, 1990.

Haft, Lloyd. *Pien Chih-lin: A Study in Modern Chinese Poetry*. Dordrecht: Foris, 1983.

Ho, Ch'i-fang. *Paths in Dreams: Selected Prose and Poetry of Ho Ch'i-fang*. Trans. Bonnie S. McDougall. St. Lucia: University of Queensland Press, 1976.

Hsu, Kai-yu. *Wen I-to*. Boston: Twayne, 1980.

Lee, Gregory. *Dai Wangshu: The Life and Poetry of a Chinese Modernist*. Hong Kong: Chinese University Press, 1989.

Lomen and Yungtzu. *Sun and Moon Collection: Selected Poems of Lomen and Yungtzu*. Trans. Angela C. Y. Jung Palandri. Taipei: Mei Ya, 1968.

Wen I-to. *Red Candle: Selected Poems*. Trans. Tao Tao Sanders. London: Kape, 1972.

Yang Lian. *Masks and Crocodile*. Trans. Mabel Lee. Sydney: University of Sydney East Asia Series, 1990.

Yang Mu and Lo Ch'ing. *The Forbidden Game and Video Poems: The Poetry of Yang Mu and Lo Ch'ing*. Trans. Joseph Allen. Seattle: University of Washington Press, 1993.

Yu Kwang-chung. *Acres of Barbed Wire: China in Daydreams and Nightmares*. Taipei: Mei Ya, 1971.

Anthologies and Special Issues

Acton, Harold, and Shih-hsiang Chen, eds. and trans. *Modern Chinese Poetry*. London: Duckworth Press, 1936.

Alley, Rewi, comp. and trans. *Light and Shadow along a Great Road: An Anthology of Modern Chinese Poetry*. Beijing: New World Press, 1984.

Barmé, Geremy, and John Minford, eds. *Seeds of Fire: Chinese Voices of Conscience*. New York: Hill and Wang, 1988.

Birch, Cyril, ed. *Anthology of Chinese Literature*. Vol. 2: *From the Fourteenth Century to the Present Day*. New York: Grove, 1972.

Cheung, Dominic, trans. and ed. *The Isle Full of Noises: Modern Chinese Poetry from Taiwan*. New York: Columbia University Press, 1986.

Ch'i, Pang-yuan, ed. and comp. *An Anthology of Contemporary Chinese Literature: Taiwan, 1949–1974*. 2 vols. Taipei: National Institute for Compilation and Translation, 1975.

Droogenbroodt, Germain, and Peter Stinson, eds. and trans. *China China: Contemporary Poetry from Taiwan, Republic of China*. Ninove, Belgium: Point Books, 1986.

Duke, Michael S., ed. *Contemporary Chinese Literature: An Anthology of Post-Mao Fiction and Poetry*. Armonk, N.Y.: M. E. Sharpe, 1985.

Finkel, Donald, with Carolyn Kizer, trans. *A Splintered Mirror: Chinese Poetry from the Democracy Movement*. San Francisco: Northpoint, 1991.

Hsu, Kai-yu, ed. and trans. *Twentieth-Century Chinese Poetry: An Anthology*. Ithaca, N.Y.: Cornell University Press, 1963.

Ing, Nancy, ed. and trans. *New Voices: Stories and Poems by Young Chinese Writers*. Taipei: Heritage Press, 1961.

———. *Summer Glory: A Collection of Contemporary Chinese Poetry*. San Francisco: Chinese Materials Center, 1982.

Link, Perry, ed. *Stubborn Weeds: Popular and Controversial Chinese Literature after the Cultural Revolution*. Bloomington: Indiana University Press, 1983.

Morin, Edward, et al., eds. and trans. *The Red Azalea: Chinese Poetry since the Cultural Revolution*. Honolulu: University of Hawaii Press, 1990.

Nieh, Hualing, ed. *Literature of the Hundred Flowers*. Vol. 2: *Poetry and Fiction*. New York: Columbia University Press, 1981.

Palandri, Angela C. Y. Jung, with Robert J. Bertholf, eds. and trans. *Modern Verse from Taiwan*. Berkeley: University of California Press, 1972.

Pang, Bingjun, and John Minford, with Seán Golden, eds. and trans. *One Hundred Chinese Poems: Chinese-English*. Hong Kong: Commercial Press, 1987.

Payne, Robert, ed. *Contemporary Chinese Poetry*. London: Routledge, 1947.

Rexroth, Kenneth, and Ling Chung, eds. and trans. *Women Poets of China*. New York: New Directions, 1972.

Rosenwald, John, ed. "Smoking People: Encountering the New Chinese Poetry," *Beloit Poetry Journal* (Chapbook 19) 39.2 (Winter 1988–89).

Siu, Helen F., and Zelda Stern, eds. *Mao's Harvest: Voices from China's New Generation*. New York: Oxford University Press, 1983.

Soong, Stephen C., and John Minford, eds. *Trees on the Mountain: An Anthology of New Chinese Writing*. Hong Kong: Chinese University Press, 1984.

Yang Mu, ed., "Taiwan Poetry," *Micromegas* 5.3 (1972).

Yip, Wai-lim, ed. and trans. *Modern Chinese Poetry: Twenty Poets from the Republic of China, 1955–1965*. Iowa City: University of Iowa Press, 1970.

———. *Lyrics from Shelters: Modern Chinese Poetry, 1930–1950*. New York: Garland Press, 1991.

Yu, Kwang-chung, ed. and trans. *New Chinese Poetry*. Taipei: Heritage, 1960.

Critical Studies of Modern Chinese Poetry

Lin, Julia. *Essays on Contemporary Chinese Poetry*. Athens: Ohio University Press, 1985.

———. *Modern Chinese Poetry: An Introduction*. Seattle: University of Washington Press, 1972.

Yeh, Michelle. *Modern Chinese Poetry: Theory and Practice since 1917*. New Haven: Yale University Press, 1991.

Index